"It was seven twenty-eight a.m., 1st July,
1916. There was a sudden, uncanny silence,
as the artillery lifted its bombardment
from the first-line German trenches to the
rear support-system. Thousands of men
were looking at their watches ..."
The Battle of the Somme – the most
terrible catastrophe in the history of the
British army – lasted four and a half
months. The British Army suffered more
than 400,000 casualties, more than in the
whole course of World War II; the French
lost 200,000; the Germans about half a
million. The Somme was the crowning folly
of the generals whose tactics Wavell later
described as "mass butchery". For Britain
it meant the death of a whole generation of
fighting men.
Here, for the first time since 1919, is an
unofficial account of the military
incompetence which led to the disaster, and
an unforgettable picture of the courage and
endurance of the men at the front.

Also by Brian Gardner
and available in Sphere Books

MAFEKING
A Victorian Legend

published in Great Britain in 1961
Cassell & Co. Ltd.

Brian Gardner 1961

st Sphere Books edition, 1968

Africa:	Kenya, Uganda, Tanzania, Zambia, Malawi: Thomas Nelson & Sons Ltd., Kenya; South.Africa, Rhodesia: Thomas Nelson & Sons (Africa) (Pty) Ltd., Johannesburg; Ghana, Nigeria, Sierra Leone: Thomas Nelson & Sons Ltd., Nigeria; Liberia: Wadih M. Captan; Angola, Mozambique: Electoliber Limitada, Angola; Zambia: Kingstons (North) Ltd.
Australia:	Thomas Nelson (Australia) Ltd.
Austria:	Danubia-Auslieferung
Bahamas:	Calypso Distributors Ltd.
Belgium:	Agence et Messageries de la Presse, S.A.
Canada:	Thomas Nelson & Sons (Canada) Ltd.
Caribbean:	Roland I. Khan (Trinidad)
Denmark:	Sven Gade, Scandinavian Book Wholesale
France:	Librairie Etrangere, Hachette
Germany:	Distropa Buchvertrieb
Gibraltar:	Estogans Agencies Ltd.
Greece:	Hellenic Distribution Agency Ltd.
Holland:	Van Ditmar
Hong Kong:	Western Publications Distribution Agency (H.K) Ltd.
Israel:	Steimatzky's Agency Ltd.
Iran:	I.A.D.A.
Iraq:	Dar Alaruba Universal Distribution Co.
Kuwait & Gulf States:	Farajalla Press Agency
Lebanon:	The Levant Distributors Co.
Malaysia, Singapore and Brunei:	Marican & Sons (Malaysia) (Sdn) Berhad
Malta:	Progress Press Co. Ltd.
New Zealand:	Hodder & Stoughton Ltd.
Portugal:	Electroliber Limitada
South America:	Colombia: Libreria Central Chile: Libreria Studio Mexico and Central America: Libreria Britanica Peru: Librerias ABC Venezuela: Distribuidora Santiago
Spain:	Comercial Atheneum
Sweden:	Importbokhandeln
Switzerland:	Friedr. Daeniker
Thailand:	The Pramuansarn Publishing House
Turkey:	Librairie Hachette
West Indies:	Barbados: Wayfarer Bookstore

TRADE MARK

Printed in Great Britain by
C. Nicholls & Company Ltd.

The Big Push
The Somme 1916

BRIAN GARDNER

Fir
by

©

F:

SPHERE BOOKS LIMITED LONDON

CONTENTS

Prologue: Over the Top

Chapter		*Page*
1	The Old Army	11
2	The Decision	16
3	Verdun	21
4	The Amateurs	27
5	The Old Front Line	32
6	The Plan	35
7	Preparations	43
8	The Home Front	60
9	'Jerry'	62
10	Making it Easy	68
11	Getting on Parade	71
12	The Push	79
13	The French	99
14	Across No Man's Land	102
15	'Carry on!'	105
16	'Tanks'	128
17	A Vital Error	133
18	Mud	139
19	Red Tabs	145
20	The Ancre	151
21	The Allies and the Enemy	153
22	'Tommy Atkins'	156
23	'Napoo!'	160
	Bibliography	168
	Notes	170
	Index	177

LIST OF MAPS

The Somme, 1916   84
The front line, 1916-17   164
The Somme and Verdun, 1916   166

ACKNOWLEDGEMENTS

I AM indebted to the following:

Messrs. William Kimber and Co., for an extract from *The War Diaries of Albert I*; Odhams Press, for extracts from *The World Crisis* by Sir Winston Churchill; the Controller of H.M. Stationery Office, for extracts from *History of the Great War, Military Operations, France and Belgium, 1916*; Messrs. Jonathan Cape, for extracts from *A Brass Hat in No Man's Land* by F. P. Crozier; Messrs. Michael Joseph, for extracts from *The Men I Killed* by F. P. Crozier; Messrs. Peter Davies for an extract from *A Subaltern's War* by Charles Edmonds; Messrs. R. H. Johns for extracts from *Going Across* by M. St. Helier Evans; The Beaverbrook Foundations for extracts from *The War Memoirs* of David Lloyd George; Messrs. Faber and Faber for extracts from *Up to Mametz* by L. W. Griffith; Messrs. Jonathan Cape for extracts from *The Somme, and the Coward* by A. D. Gristwood; Lord Haig and Messrs. Eyre and Spottiswoode for extracts from *The Private Papers of Douglas Haig* edited by Robert Blake; Messrs. Arthur Barker for an extract from *The Land-Locked Lake* by A. A. Hanbury-Sparrow; Messrs. J. M. Dent and Sons for extracts from *A Subaltern on the Somme* by 'Mark VII'; The Society of Authors and Dr. John Masefield, O.M., for extracts from *The Battle of the Somme* by John Masefield; Messrs. William Collins Sons and Co. for an extract from Lord Montgomery's *Memoirs*; Messrs. Faber and Faber for extracts from *Memoirs of an Infantry Officer* by Siegfried Sassoon; Messrs. Macdonald and Co. for an extract from *The Golden Virgin* by Henry Williamson; Edmund Blunden for an extract from *Undertones of War* published by Cobden-Sanderson.

'The battle of the Somme was a great triumph for the genius of British military leadership.'

J. H. Boraston and *G. A. B. Dewar*, 1922

PROLOGUE

OVER THE TOP

EVERYONE who was there remembers it as a quite startlingly beautiful summer's morning. There was not a cloud to be seen in the sky; the early morning sun shone down on the fields of northern France like a blessing. Although not long after seven o'clock, it was already very hot.

Above the thundering of the guns, the distant calls of trains could sometimes be heard. Across No Man's Land, facing the British trenches, wild flowers were scattered among the unruly grass and scrub. In some parts there was a thin, grey stubble left from the last harvest in 1914. Partly hidden by the grass and shell holes were the scattered debris of two years of raiding. Beyond this stretch of No Man's Land was a long, gentle slope. Along this were the German trenches and dug-outs.

It was seven twenty-eight a.m., 1 July 1916.

There was a sudden, uncanny silence, as the artillery lifted its bombardment from the first-line German trenches to the rear support-system. Thousands of men were looking at their watches.

At seven-thirty precisely whistles blew all along the line of British trenches. Young officers leapt up, gesticulating, shouting, and pointing towards the German positions. Suddenly the packed trenches changed from stillness to turmoil. Men clambered up ladders, were hit on the parapet, and fell back on those behind. Some cheered. Some screamed. Some remained tight-lipped and silent. Some laughed hysterically.

Fourteen divisions of British troops, along a front of eighteen miles, went over the top, many of them for the first time. The vast majority of them had been civilians two years previously. Before this, their greatest caper had been to cut a trim figure on roller skates. Now they were to walk into almost certain death or injury.

Coming out of the trenches and through the gaps in their own wire in file, the battalions soon strung out in long lines, each man about an arm's distance from the next. Bayonets glinted in the sun.

The Germans sent down an enormous flail of concentrated machine-gun fire. It hummed and whirred through the air around the lines of steadily advancing troops. It thudded home into their sweating bodies, through equipment straps and khaki cloth. In a few minutes the first waves were annihilated. But wave upon wave came pouring out of the trenches to take the place of the fallen. They surged over the broken ground at a steady walking pace, loaded with sixty-six pounds of equipment around them, and a few gulps of luke-warm soup and a tot of rum inside their bellies. Nowhere could they see the enemy. But they knew he was up there on the ridge, as they could hear and feel him well enough.

Over the roar and crash of battle, cheering could be heard from some of the battalions. Others broke before the murderous hail of machine-gun bullets and began to stumble back. A few got as far as the German wire; as they got entangled in it the Germans used rifle fire to kill them off one by one. Wounded soldiers inextricably caught up in the wire, which had barbs two inches long, vainly screamed for help and attempted to tear off their clothes. Few escaped. A naked man was seen running about in the middle of No Man's Land, yelling incomprehensibly at the top of his voice. Most, however, never got as far as the wire. They lay in No Man's Land as shells exploded among them, and bullets scythed through the deadly air above their heads.

Nostrils sickened by the scent of explosive fumes, ears numbed with noise, senses bewildered and insulted, brains half paralysed with shock, thousands of men lay there in the grass, among their groaning comrades. Around them lay another twenty thousand British soldiers, all dead. Fathers, sons, brothers, loved-ones, who had gone to the slaughter-house because they were told to do so; because they genuinely felt a need to get to grips with the Hun; because everyone else did; because they were scared not to; because they did not know what was waiting for them.

The sun shone down on the basking, smoking battlefield. Slowly, painfully, some of the men lying there began to wonder what had gone wrong. ...

CHAPTER ONE

THE OLD ARMY

BEFORE the world went to war in 1914 the River Somme was a minor placid waterway of northern France. It meandered gently through Picardy, through a broad valley; westwards and north-wards towards the English Channel. Men fished on its banks. Lovers nestled in the reeds, and punts slipped in and out of the complicated channels. On the uplands to either side villages lay in the folds of the undulating slopes. A contented, canny breed of peasants made an adequate living from the land and from rich, productive orchards. It was a countryside of singular rural beauty, not unlike parts of Hampshire. The Somme watered it all; the fat orchards, the rich cornfields, the marshy meadows. Rows of tall, sentinel poplars lined the Route Nationale. Carts creaked down the lanes to Bapaume, Thiepval, and Albert. Life was a matter of sowing, reaping, and gathering the harvest; of apple-picking, of children's laughter, of fish hiding near the banks, of the sound of church bells drifting over the valley on still Sunday mornings. It was not the most well-known area in France. Few visitors came upon it. Many local families had never left it, had never seen the sea, and had visited Paris only once in a generation.

The uplands were almost solid chalk, and from them the view extended for up to three miles. On some of the slopes were several thick woods. On Sunday afternoons young couples would stroll shyly into the woods called Delville and Mam-etz. . . .

*

To those lying in No Man's Land on 1 July 1916, it must have seemed a long time ago to the days before the war; a different age, recalled like some half-forgotten dream. But whatever had gone wrong had started then.

The men who planned and directed the Battle of the Somme, who painstakingly prepared for it and dreamed of it for six months before, were the cream of the pre-war army; products of a military age far removed from that which existed on the Western Front in 1916. The army in which they had risen to

11

high authority was very different from the army in which they eventually found themselves commanders in a European war. . . .

One of its most serious defects was low pay, which hampered recruitment of the better type of officers and men. Even until 1900 there was also far too much leave, which made for inefficiency. Officers were accustomed in some regiments to as much as six months' leave in a year. Many of these officers had failed at Oxford or Cambridge, or both; they were not very bright, there was not much else to be done with them, so they were sent into the army.

For more than forty years the cavalry had been the stronger wing of the army. Tradition was strict; much of it lasted up to the war, and some of it managed, in a macabre fashion, to cling grotesquely on through the bloodbath. To get married while a subaltern, for instance, was in the very poorest taste (it meant that the officer in question paid only half the normal mess subscription). Subalterns were not expected to talk at dinner. Even if they had wished to do so, to converse would not have been easy, for many subjects were forbidden. Religion was out of the question; politics were equally unacceptable; military tactics were 'shop' and thus in bad taste (one might cause embarrassment by showing up someone else's ignorance); ladies were not to be mentioned by name. Lisping flourished. There was also a widespread habit of interjecting every now and again, preferably in mid-sentence, 'haw-haw' – loudly and slowly, for no discernible reason.

Officers and men normally disliked, and often despised, each other. No one got any nearer to understanding how to employ modern weapons in war. No one thought, apparently, about the effectiveness of a large force of cavalry, such as Britain proudly possessed, against a handful of machine-guns. Tactics, in fact, were interesting, but they were not to interfere with war. There was little point, for example, in surprising a group of dervishes when you were to charge them on horseback. That would spoil half the sport.

At fairly frequent intervals a regiment or two set off to fire a few shots at those of the Queen's subjects who did not appreciate the *Pax Britannica*. In the depths of Africa, in the heart of the Sudan, in Griqualand and on the North-West Frontier, the red coats went – with their world-famous horses, their polo ponies, and their regimental wines. And practically everyone in the army had at least one tour in India, with its memsahibs, its servants (whose extreme servility could bring out the arrogance in the most modest officer), its heat, and its pig-sticking ('I know of few delights to compare with it,' said Lord Birdwood).

After the army had been disgraced in the Boer War, there were efforts at reform. Under Haldane it became better trained and well disciplined, but the absurd customs and affectations clung on. How can you force 'wegiments' to send officers to Staff College when they believe they will learn there a lot of nonsense about politics and the Huns, and when anyway they are needed for the polo team?

And so the years went on. The subalterns became colonels. The Kaiser became an 'Emperor'. In 1914 a certain Brigadier-General Gough achieved brief notoriety at an 'incident' at the Curragh camp in Ireland, when some calvary officers looked like resigning over a point of principle. The nation was shocked. To show the army where it stood an order was issued saying: 'An officer or soldier is forbidden in future to ask for assurances as to orders which he may be required to obey.' Later that summer there were extensive manoeuvres on Salisbury Plain; the lances glistened in the sun, and the officers' wives gasped at the magnificence of it all. There were vague and complicated happenings in Central Europe that few people could understand. In August the Kaiser marched his army into Belgium, threatening the Channel Ports. Britain went to war; there was cheering in the streets.

The British Expeditionary Force, of a hundred thousand men, thanks to Haldane, was ready and waiting. It would not be quite like fighting the Afghans, of course, but it would not take long. Most people had great confidence in the Commander-in-Chief, Sir John French, a brilliant cavalryman.

Few realized that war had become a national, not a specialized, thing; that improved education and communications would make it an affair of interest to entire populations; that scientific invention would introduce all kinds of hitherto undreamed of weapons – such as submarines and gas; that armies would soon be of such a size that entirely new tactical thinking would be required.

That the attack might come through Belgium had been known to the French command since 1911, when General Michel had made his preparations for just such an eventuality. The French military experts, however, disagreed with him. He was replaced by General Joffre, a man with wide experience in colonial wars in the East, in Africa (at Timbuctoo), and in Madagascar. Owing to the rejection of the Michel plan, and the inadequacy of the subsequent Joffre plan, in 1914 the French reeled back on Paris. During the general withdrawal the British force met the Germans at Mons and acquitted itself well. After a recovery by the allies, the line was extended till it reached the beach near Ostend at one end and the Swiss frontier near Belfort at the other. This line across the heart of Western Europe, printed on countless maps, became as familiar to people of the time as the reflection of their own faces. Stalemate immediately followed. The two sides were locked in each other's grip; push as they might, they hardly managed to move.

In England meanwhile, Lord Kitchener became Minister of War on Haldane's advice, although many people tried to persuade Haldane to return to the War Office himself. But he was at the time violently attacked in the Press and elsewhere for wrongly suspected pro-German sympathies. 'K', as Kitchener was called, realized that the war would last several years, and to make sure that it would be won he made his main task the recruiting of a great popular Army. Men were signed on, slowly at first, but later coming in streams, for three years 'or the duration'. The famous poster appeared; so did white feathers. The hit song of the day was Phyllis Dare singing 'Oh, we don't want to lose you, but we think you ought to go'. Long queues at the recruiting offices became common. Men, often urged on by excited women, were anxious to get to the front, and to prove their manliness.

Some men, however, now started looking farther on the map than the 'Front'. They wondered why the enemy could not be defeated in the Balkans, where so many nations were uncommitted, waiting only to discover the eventual winner. They wished to advance up the comparatively unprotected part of the German Empire, instead of fighting its army on its own choice of field. These minds, led by Winston Churchill, were given their chance, although the army had no confidence in their ideas. The force that landed at Gallipoli on 25 April 1915 failed to get clear of the beaches. The supporters of grand strategy, of a bold use of imaginative measures, never recovered from this disaster; which had a great bearing on the strategy for 1916.

Casualties were proving much heavier than had seemed possible in that happy August in 1914, and in January 1916 conscription for bachelors was introduced. Lloyd George, a man with a reputation for getting things done, was made Minister of Munitions; not only was there a shortage of men, there was also a shortage of shells. For the French and British Generals had meanwhile been getting on with their own ideas of how the war should be won. These consisted, in defence, of preserving every inch of ground, or, in attack, of hurling large numbers of troops against the enemy line after an artillery barrage had 'prepared the way'. No successes had been achieved, and the line remained substantially as it was. The French suffered most. The British fought heroically, but to little avail, at Neuve Chapelle, at Ypres ('Wipers'), and, in September 1915, at Loos; the last-named being a catastrophically mismanaged attempt to break the line. The Germans suffered least of all. Clearly, greater efforts would have to be made before the deadlock was broken, and it seemed that Sir John French was not the man to direct them.

At seven p.m. on 10 December 1915, General Sir Douglas Haig, the commander of the army which had recently been mauled at Loos, received a letter from the Prime Minister, Asquith. It was enclosed in three envelopes, and it read:

> Sir John French has placed in my hands his resignation of the office of Commander-in-Chief of the Forces in France. Subject to the King's approval, I have the pleasure of proposing to you that you should be his successor. I am satisfied that this is the best choice that could be made in the interests of the Army and the Country.

In England, Kitchener's great army of eager civilians was parading on bleak, wintry barrack squares. In France, Generals Joffre and Haig were in command. The cast was ready. The drama was about to begin.

CHAPTER TWO

THE DECISION

On 6 December 1915, an allied military conference was assembled to discuss operations for the coming year. As usual on these occasions, it was held at the headquarters of General Joffre, a magnificent château at Chantilly. It was decided that the four powers, France, Russia, Britain, and Italy, should deliver four attacks, as nearly simultaneously as possible, with their maximum forces on their respective fronts. Before these attacks got under way, the Austro-German forces were to be ceaselessly pounded and harried by subsidiary attacks. Only minimum forces were to be allotted to 'secondary' theatres of war. This agreement reflected a remarkable success of Joffre in getting his way; the plan was little more than an endorsement of his own desires. As a result of the meeting the British War Committee directed that an offensive was to be carried out in the following year in the greatest possible strength, the plan to be left to the army commanders in France. It was decided that the Western Front was to remain the primary theatre of war.

This left Joffre and the newly appointed Sir Douglas Haig to detail the plan for the offensive. Joffre's idea was to stage an enormous attack on a front of sixty miles, across the River Somme. The British were soon to have four armies north of the Somme, and their section of the front covered about eighty miles. Although comparatively small in the total frontage, it was a section of great importance, faced by some of the best German troops.

The Somme, in fact, was suggested as the place of attack by Joffre, in a note to Haig, as early as 30 December 1915. Said Joffre: 'The ground is in many places favourable to the development of a powerful offensive.'

Haig preferred an attack in Flanders, to combine with a Naval landing. A strategic objective, he said, could be pursued there. The enemy's line, possibly, could be rolled up. The coast could be reached, and the nervy politicians at home would feel happier if an attempt was being made to get the Hun right away from the coast across the Channel. We learn from Charteris, Haig's intelligence officer, however, that 'the operations section [of G.H.Q.] are all for the Somme, on account of it being much easier ground to attack over'. Haig argued hard with Joffre, but Joffre, as was his custom, won. As the *Official History of the War* says, Haig had an 'unvarying principle of meeting the French wishes wherever possible'. It states categorically that the Somme battle 'was fought, like the Battle of Loos, not only on the ground and the day chosen by the French, but at the very hour selected by them; and that neither place, nor date or time was what the British Commander-in-Chief would have chosen had he been free to do so'. Haig, however, got a chance to test his Flanders theory the following year.

It seems that the main reason for the Somme sector of the front being chosen was the fact that there the British and French armies met. The French were to the south of the river; the British to the north of it. Joffre felt that it would be a good thing for the two nations to go into the assault together, side by side. But knowing full well the strength of the German position there, he also knew that attrition was likely to be the inevitable result of a prolonged attack.

Joffre asked for preliminary attacks before the main assault in order, he said, to wear the enemy down and weaken his resistance to the final blow. He wished for one such attack, for some reason, on 20 April precisely. Another should follow in May. Haig, however, preferred to conserve his armies for the one great effort. His troops were by no means fully trained or prepared, and Haig was a meticulous trainer. He persuaded Joffre, during the spring and early summer, that he could not afford to threaten his preparations in this way. Joffre remained unconvinced; but there were no small-scale attacks.

By 11 February the plan seemed to be decided. As Charteris wrote in his diary: 'The main attack, French and British, is to be astride the Somme, us to the north, they to the south.'

On 14 March in the course of further discussions on the coming allied attack, Haig visited Paris. He lunched at the Crillon, and afterwards strolled with Charteris as far as the Invalides. There he insisted on seeing Napoleon's tomb, despite the fact that the place was closed. After a good deal of fuss, he was eventually admitted. In the huge marble hall, beneath the high dome, the little Scotsman stood and quietly contemplated the tomb of the great Bonaparte.

At this time an argument was raging as to the timing of the offensive. The assault was clearly impossible to arrange for the spring. Neither the British armies, nor the Russians who were to attack simultaneously in the east, would be ready by that early date. The month of July was being mentioned as the likely time by 14 February. As the weeks passed, the date of the coming battle was changed backwards and forwards from mid-June to the beginning of July; Joffre always trying to bring it forward, Haig struggling to delay it.

Joffre's intention was to 'wear the enemy down'; to crush him with sheer weight of force and shell, to weaken his will to win. Haig had no better idea, apart from Flanders. His instructions were to comply with Joffre's wishes, within reason. This seemed within reason. He could see nothing particularly wrong with the Somme plan, it was just that he felt the Flanders plan better suited British interests. He accepted Joffre's plan; but there is no reason to think that he *had* to. In December Kitchener had written to him: 'I wish you distinctly to understand that your command is an independent one, and that you will in no case come under the orders of any Allied General.'

Winston Churchill later observed: 'The policy of the French and British Commanders had selected as the point for their offensive what was undoubtedly the strongest and most perfectly defended position in the world.' This position, wrote D. C. Somervell, 'surpassed in strength anything ever seen before in the history of war'. The casual, arbitrary way in which the Battle of the Somme, in which it must have been known that thousands would lose their lives, was decided on, is one of the greatest horrors of the story of the battle.

It is often stated by defenders of Haig that he only fought on the Somme in order to save the war, by drawing German attention away from Verdun, where the French were (as will be seen) at the point of collapse. In fact, however, the battle had been decided on at Chantilly, on a cold, wintry afternoon, before the German command had even launched their offensive at Verdun.

Throughout the early discussions it was always understood that the French were to take the major share of the assault. It was later agreed that there were to be thirty-nine French divisions under the command of General Foch, and twenty-five to thirty British divisions from the Third and Fourth Armies, under Generals Sir Edmund Allenby and Sir Henry Rawlinson respectively.

There were similar characteristics between the two Commanders-in-Chief, many of them fine ones. Joffre was, indeed, a kind of exaggerated, French Haig. They were both products of a national desire for military idols that were strong, silent, mighty men of action. They even had certain physical similarities. Their chins were thrusting, powerful, and confident. Their foreheads were narrow and thin. Conventional soldiers, they had no mental equipment to solve military problems outside their own experience. They had not been trained for original thought. But look as some of the more dissatisfied politicians did for someone to replace them, there was no one on the horizon even who seemed to promise any better.

Joffre was sixty-three years old. An engineer officer, he had been a young lieutenant in the siege of Paris in 1870. He was now, as Lloyd George pointed out, 'the virtual dictator of France'. He occupied a position in the minds of Frenchmen rather like that of Kitchener in the minds of Englishmen. He was supposed to be infallible. No government felt powerful enough to depose him, although many politicians had already lost faith in him. They feared the public outcry that the forced resignation of a national hero would bring.

'Papa' Joffre had become almost unmanageable. He was insolent. He browbeat politicians, and demanded of Ministers. Whenever he heard of criticism, he murmured with sad resignation, 'Pauvre Joffre'. He was mainly responsible for the military policy of the allies in 1916, and had been since the beginning of the war. It seemed that no one could stand up to him, and Haig, firm and stubborn though he was, was no match for him.

Joffre's blunders in 1914, at the time of the German invasion, would have been enough to finish a less composed man. The victory of the Marne saved him and France, although little credit was due to him personally, and with considerable aplomb he continued to direct the fortunes of the allies as if nothing had happened. He was interested in only one theatre of war – the Western Front – his natural ambition being to get every German off French soil.

Douglas Haig was fifty-four years old, and the British military hero of the day. He had been educated at Clifton and at Oxford, where he failed to take a degree. He had found Sandhurst more to his liking. He had the fetish of cleanliness customary to one of his background; an excellent rider, he had no unconventional views or habits. He had passed out first of his year.

Before long he had become adjutant of the 7th Hussars, which, thanks to him, had soon had one of the most consistent polo teams in the British army. He had secured the friendship of the Commander-in-Chief of the day, the Duke of Cambridge, and had then become known to the Prince of Wales, later King George V; prince and ambitious soldier became friends. By 1904, when he had been appointed Major-General, he was in quite an exceptional position, having a closer ear to royalty than any of his superiors. In 1905 he had been a guest at Windsor, where he met one of the Queen's ladies-in-waiting, and his marriage proposal had been accepted by her two days later.

In a society where it was better to be a good average than gifted, his progress was inevitable. He had written a paper in which he noted the 'greatly increased power of action possessed by cavalry'. And in 1907 he had written a book on the role of cavalry, in which he believed passionately. Called *Cavalry Studies*, it had showed considerable knowledge of the subject and referred to Moltke, the cavalry of the Army of the Potomac in 1863, and esoteric Russian and French military professors.

By 1910, when he had been promoted Lieutenant-General, Haig had become a set, rigid being. His well-polished boots creaking, his eyes steady, fearless, and expressionless, his moustache immaculately trimmed, he was the superman of the modern army. Competent, well-connected, studious in military matters, sober, religious, patriotic – it would have been difficult to fault him in his own context. Given luck, it seemed that nothing could prevent the fulfilment of his ambition – the command of a British army in the field in a European war.

Soon after the war began, he had started writing to the King complaining of Sir John French's command. He had seen French's many failings only too clearly. On a visit to London late in 1915 he had campaigned ceaselessly for his chief's removal, telling Haldane and the King of French's 'obstinacy and conceit'. He had written in his diary: 'I had come to the conclusion that it is not fair to the Empire to retain French in command on this the main battle front.' He had also written to Kitchener in similar terms.

These, then, were the two key figures on the scene; Joffre and Haig. But all thoughts of allied Generals, and of the coming offensive on the Somme, were now momentarily put in second place. The Germans had launched an enormous and crucial attack, on the fortifications of the small but ancient French town called Verdun.

CHAPTER THREE

VERDUN

EARLY in January 1916, French intelligence had begun to refer to Verdun as the most likely place for a forthcoming German attack. Falkenhayn, who had become German Commander-in-Chief after the failure of the attempt to snatch victory in 1914, had, in order to justify himself, to break the stalemate. Knowing that the French would defend every inch of ground at Verdun, a place of little strategic importance, but emotionally vital to the French, it was there that he had chosen to make his attack. The intention was to exhaust the French by whittling away their manpower. Although this was known to the French, little was done to prepare for a lengthy battle. Joffre himself, who seldom left his cumbersome administrative and planning machine at Chantilly, was quite undisturbed. This was to be expected. His complete placidity in the face of all kinds of threats and imminent collapses was one of the reasons why he was still in command. He was, invariably, so reassuring. Only the more junior officers, the colonels in the field, likely to lose their lives in battle, were apprehensive as the weeks went on and the German preparations became more obvious. These men included Deputies of the French Parliament, now serving soldiers. They sent back reports to Ministers in Paris complaining of a lack of preparedness. Very little was done, except that their names were noted by the resentful staff at Chantilly.

At four o'clock in the morning of 21 February a 14-inch shell exploded in the Archbishop's Palace at Verdun. It was the signal for battle. A brief but shatteringly powerful bombardment followed, and in the early morning three German Army Corps advanced on the apex of the French salient. During the succeeding weeks the French line was steadily pushed back, a few hundred yards being regained one day only to be lost again the next. The casualties on both sides were heavy. There is a story that the Kaiser himself came to see this pounding away of the French army. He is said to have sat in the cellar of a building on the reverse side of a slope near to the front. There, in what he considered reasonable safety, he was able to watch his countrymen die, using a periscope up a chimney.

On the French side, General Pétain was in charge of the defence. An inspiring, tough, immensely patriotic soldier, he conceived his duty a simple one. The German advance must be stemmed. It was unthinkable to give ground, even if that were strategically wise. (The idea that Verdun could be turned into victory for the French, by a steady, controlled withdrawal, sapping up the German strength, and ensnaring them into a dangerous noose, *did* occur to some strategists, but they were 'amateurs' in Paris.) Pétain's policy was perfectly straightforward: not an inch more must be given up. If he had been a German agent, his strategy could hardly have suited Falkenhayn better.

Despite the fact that the French had been aware of the coming attack, little had been done to bring up reserves. The Germans steadily pushed on. The situation was critical. The dreadful, smoking belly of Verdun seemed unquenchable; in all, sixty-five French divisions made the journey in the three thousand trucks that went to and from the line every day. But it was becoming clear, as winter turned to a blossomless, battleground spring, and spring became what looked like being a fine, dry summer of turquoise blue skies, that the French soldiers were beginning to expect little more than death in battle.

Rumours swept France. They even reached Douglas Haig. The situation was nothing like as serious as it was to become the following year, but discipline was weakening, especially among the Colonial troops. The word 'mutiny' was frequently being heard at the front. There were strange stories of battalions disappearing into thin air; of soldiers parleying with the Germans across No Man's Land; of summary shootings of numbers of Frenchmen, including some officers, by their own countrymen on charges of cowardice and mutiny. There was, in fact, a serious outbreak of low morale in the French Army. At the moment it was controllable. Affected units were being sent back, miles behind the line, to be re-formed. But such things could spread, insidiously, like a dangerous rash. Secret service agents in the ranks began to report that the average soldier would not take very much more of the war. Letters sent home from the front, read by the censor, gave a similar view.

The French army had, till now, taken the whole brunt of the war. The Russians had not lived up to expectations; the Russian 'steamroller' that was to overwhelm the Kaiser's ambitions by sheer weight of numbers was proving, until Brusilov's offensive on 4 June with a million men, somewhat elusive. The British had, in effect, spent two years producing an army on the Continental scale. Their exploits at Mons and elsewhere, hailed in the British press as decisive factors, were sideshows to the efforts of the French army.

And the French army, by early summer of 1916, was plainly discouraged and exhausted. It had been too long in the trenches, with too little leave. The ordinary soldier had continually been kept in ignorance of the object of his actions. His pay was poor, and the billets were crowded and unsatisfactory. The food, above all, was depressing – and food is of some importance to the efficiency and battle-willingness of the French solider. There was no kind of welfare organization, or even a practical system for the airing of complaints. There seemed no future to look forward to, except a life of trenches and explosives, bayonets and wire. There was a great longing to get home.

General des Vallières, liaison officer at the British H.Q. reported: 'Situation at Verdun serious. Not only men but Generals and Staff are getting tired and jumpy.'

And all the time there was resentment of the British. They seemed to be getting off lightly ; playing their traditional role of letting European allies fight their battles for them. All during that spring and early summer there was one question in the French people's minds: why don't the British do something? It's time they took a share.

The German clevely played on this feeling. In neutral countries they began making cutting remarks about the British being willing to let the French do all the fighting. These remarks were echoed in the French press, which was taking on a distinctly anti-British tone. As a sop, official French propaganda was distributed to the Paris papers about a great British offensive coming shortly ; it would take the weight off the French troops. The German High Command, of course, received all the Paris newspapers.

The Battle of Verdun, meanwhile, was continuing unabated. Little ground changed hands, but many men were dying. Every inch of soil was being desperately defended, as if the very fate of France depended on it.

Every week more and more reinforcements were arriving, collected from all parts of the front. Most of these divisions had been intended for use in the coming Somme offensive. But now the French were only concerned in holding Verdun. The pride of the Generals, to say nothing of their reputations, demanded a halt to the enemy advance.

Even the placid Joffre was showing signs of concern. Although keeping to his regular hours, and eating well, he was losing his temper at frequent intervals. And he, too, was convinced that it was about time the British did something. As usual it was some time before Joffre accepted the ideas that his inferiors had accepted before him, but now he was thoroughly depressed at the situation at Verdun.

In March Haig had taken over a further sector of the French front to relieve troops needed at Verdun. But that, it seemed, was not enough. Haig had, in fact, done this fairly willingly, as he would, indeed, do anything to prevent his being rushed into the Somme Battle before his armies and all their supplies and administration were ready for the great effort. But the more of the French line he took over, the less British divisions there were resting and training for the coming battle.

Meanwhile, the number of French divisions available for the assault had shrunk from the planned thirty-nine to eighteen (in the end only five took part). It was by now accepted that the main blow was to come from the British, and not the French as originally intended. The roles of the two nations had been reversed during the weeks and months of sledge-hammer activity at Verdun. Haig made no objection to this change of plan ; had he have done so it would have made no difference. As it happened he preferred the arrangement. His desire was to take a great British army into the field, to crush the Germans with his artillery and infantry, and to finish them off with his invincible cavalry. Clearly, it was best if the French troops, already, as he understood, thoroughly demoralized, took the minor part in the affair. He said: 'There is no doubt to my mind but that the war must be won by the Forces of the British Empire.'

On 26 May, when things at Verdun were looking hopeless, when there seemed no chance of the Germans calling off the assault, Joffre left Chantilly and went to Haig's H.Q. For an hour and a half they talked in Haig's writing-room.

Joffre pressed 'vehemently' for an early British attack. In front of Haig's staff, he lost his temper, or pretended to do so, and insinuated and railed at the British General. He said: 'The French Army will cease to exist if nothing is done till August.' 1 July was settled on as a firm date. Already agreed upon before, there was now no hope of Haig postponing the battle beyond it. This was the most stormy meeting of the war between the two commanders. At it, it seems that Joffre almost succeeded in intimidating Douglas Haig, no mean feat.

On 31 May, Poincaré, the French President, accompanied by his Prime Minister, Briand, and War Minister, together with Joffre, met Haig south of Amiens in the Presidential railway carriage. General Foch, who was to supervise the French share of the battle, was also present. Poincaré had just been to Verdun, where he had seen Pétain. He was frightened that Verdun would fall, and that French mutinies would break out on a completely uncontrollable scale. Under this overwhelming barrage of French dignitaries, Haig agreed to bring forward the date for the first attack to 25 June.

In early June, Pétain himself, a man with great faith in the Frenchman as a fighting machine, was more than worried at the state of French morale. He took to telephoning Chantilly nearly every day, begging them to press the British to start the Somme offensive. He later wrote: 'I was disturbed by these symptoms of the most serious malady that can threaten an army.' Joffre wrote in his memoirs years later that he considered Pétain at this time something of an alarmist; he seems to suggest that Pétain was in a state of unnecessary and ungentlemanly panic. Pétain recorded, however, that even the phlegmatic 'Papa' himself was 'somewhat alarmed' at the situation.

Ministers were also taking a serious view of the secret reports coming in about the low state of morale. In June, Joffre received a 'most singular telephonic communication' from the Minister of War, 'urging me to make sure that nothing delayed the British attack'. Joffre was horrified, considering this a case of inexcusable meddling in his affairs. He complained, at the first opportunity, to Briand, the Prime Minister, who confided that it had come down from the President of the Republic himself. 'Extremely embarrassing,' huffed Joffre.

On 11 June Pétain wrote to Joffre once more pleading for an immediate start to the British offensive. Joffre replied: 'The French-British action will begin almost at once.' On the 17th, at the insistence of Haig, the battle date was reset once more, this time back to 29 June.

On 23 June Pétain telephoned de Castelnau, Joffre's virtual second-in-command, at Chantilly to tell him of the desperate situation. Every available man had been thrown into the line.

The Germans were still attacking. Where was further man-power to come from? This could not go on much longer.

'I ended the conversation with these words, repeating what I had been urging day after day: "You must hurry the English attack." '

Four fresh divisions were sent to him, and he was able to counter-attack on 24 June. On the same day the British batteries at the Somme opened up their initial bombardment, to be increased on the 26th.

On 26 June, Joffre told the French Government:

On 29 June the British armies will attack on the north front of the Somme. The offensive, which will involve about half the large units which are at present in France, that is to say twenty-six divisions, will be launched along a front of twenty-five kilometres between Gommecourt and Maricourt. In order to co-operate as fully as possible in the action of the English forces and to be in a position to take advantage with them of any widespread success, I have grouped under General Foch's orders all the large units and all the heavy artillery at our disposition that our situation at Verdun has not forced us to deploy on the Meuse. In spite of the fact that I have given to General Pétain, since the beginning of this battle, a total force of sixty-five divisions, the muster of French forces for the offensive on the Somme will be imposing. The attack by General Foch will extend as a matter of fact from Maricourt to Foucaucourt, along a front of about twelve kilometres. It will involve the use of about fourteen divisions to begin with, will be undertaken on the same date as that of the British armies, and will be carried on in close conjunction with them. Thus the offensive of the Franco-British armies will be launched along a front of thirty-seven kilometres, with a total force of forty divisions. Moreover, this figure will be largely increased if, as I hope, the results of the first attack are such as to allow us to count on important successes.

But Joffre was not interested in important successes on the Somme; all he cared about was relieving the pressure on Verdun before the French army collapsed and Falkenhayn's ruthless plan achieved victory. Having initially proposed an attack upon the Somme sector because he could think of nothing better, he had now to diminish the French part in it, and to call desperately for it in order to save French prestige.

CHAPTER FOUR

THE AMATEURS

THROUGHOUT the war on the Western Front, the generals, both French and British, felt that they were fighting two battles. They were fighting the German armies before them and the politicians behind them. Occasionally a general, here and there, showed signs of being unable to accept, wholeheartedly, the general strategy. Foch was unhappy, Allenby uneasy. Plumer, at Ypres, away to the north of the Somme, showed almost as much interest in the well-being of his own troops as in the destruction of the enemy's. Rawlinson, directed to command the main assault on the Somme, was sometimes taken aback by the apparent disregard of Haig, Joffre, and their staffs for human life. But their military training always got the better of these men. They acquiesced, with seldom a murmur of discontent. Good soldiers, they obeyed orders.

The politicians, on the other hand, were split into two camps – for and against the generals. In France, there were Briand and many junior politicians (most of whom had personal experience of trench warfare), against them. In England, there were Lloyd George and Churchill, joined at times by that bewildered soldier, Kitchener, who managed to keep a foot in both camps. Arthur Balfour also sided with the 'amateurs', as Haig called them, on the Somme issue. He observed: 'The French are short of men; yet they want to do something which would reduce their numbers still more.' Later, he turned sides and supported the Generals. F. E. Smith (Lord Birkenhead) was another in the Churchill group.

Churchill was the prime mover of a breakaway from the statemate of France and Flanders. His eager mind, accepting nothing, saw the map of Europe as a whole, not just a section of it. But in 1916 Churchill was one of the most unpopular men in Britain, not by any means for the last time. For a while he served at the Front (as Lieutenant-Colonel of the 6th Royal Scots Fusiliers), where he was duly horrified, and painted some macabre, and for him uncharacteristic, scenes of the area behind the lines. He served a spell in the trenches, where he successfully deloused his battalion, and had a tin bath, good brandy, and cigars brought up to his dug-out. But after four months he became sullen and depressed, and spent hours contemplating on mechanical ways of overcoming the stalemate in the trenches. In May 1916 he returned to London.

Lloyd George, although, like Kitchener, a supporter of Gallipoli, was not directly responsible for it. He continued to fight against the Western Front as the main operational zone of the war. He was a great supporter of the Salonika campaign, in which an Anglo-French expeditionary force was engaged. Here an attempt was being made to advance northwards through the Balkans, where forces sympathetic to the Allies, such as the Serbs, could eventually help to take Austria and Germany from their least protected quarter.

But, like Gallipoli, Salonika suffered from a lack of interest of the military chiefs. It seemed incomprehensible to them that anyone could hope to beat the Germans by not facing their army on the battlefield and defeating it when the two opposing forces clashed. The principles that had stood at Agincourt were still valid.

Lloyd George, a disappointing ally for Churchill, was always a little overawed by Haig. He found it easy enough to criticize, one might almost say vilify him, in writing, but when the time came he gave way. He was usually overruled by his ambition; it often got the better of him. There might be bloody, useless battles on the way, but there were also men to keep in with, other men being pushed aside, gaps to fill, and that decrepit old house in Downing Street waiting around the corner.

Despite the fact that Lloyd George later made it clear that he detested Haig almost as soon as he met him, and despised his mind and abilities, he wrote to him on 8 February after a visit to the front:

> The visit, if you will permit me to say so, left on my mind a great impression of things being gripped in that sphere of operations; and whether we win through or whether we fail, I have a feeling that all which the assiduity, the care, and the trained thought of a great soldier can accomplish, is being done.

Before the Somme, while Minister of Munitions, Lloyd George's action was limited to casting continual aspersions on the coming battle. Occasionally he told the cabinet of his grave misgivings. He was thoroughly suspicious of the military, later even suggesting the possibility of a junta. Nevertheless, during the spring and summer he got on with producing the munitions that Haig needed for the battle.

By 1916, Kitchener was stumbling through the war as best he could. The problems emerging from it were of a kind he could not understand. He had gained great popularity and a reputation for military genius, through his exploits against half-armed natives in various parts of the late Queen's Empire. With an average mind, neither particularly dull nor imaginative, he was just the kind of man to have risen to the top of the army. He had not offended anybody by having too much brain, but on the other hand he could size up a situation and write a sensible report. Most of the politicians were fond of him; some were rather sorry for him. The trouble was, he was a nuisance. He knew that something was expected of him, and he struggled to produce a shaft of genius that would solve the matter. But no shafts of genius ever emerged from Lord Kitchener. Through his shrewdness, however, an army was ready on a continental scale, when called upon.

Kitchener's last months at the War Office were an embarrassment to everyone except, possibly, himself. Sir William Robertson, the C.I.G.S., had most of the powers he wished for. When he went down into the icy depths with H.M.S. *Hampshire*, on his way to a fool's errand in Russia, the cabinet had got rid of him more finally than it had intended. Before his departure, however, he had made plain his mistrust of the coming battle for the Somme; Lloyd George has stated that 'K' was opposed to it. The day he embarked on the *Hampshire* was, by a strange chance of fate, the day on which the last of his new army left for France and the training grounds behind the Somme.

Supporting the generals were many people who believed that the best way they could serve their country, was to give the generals what they asked, and provide verbal support, supplies, men, and every kind of encouragement. To them it seemed disgraceful, almost an act of a traitor, to make difficulties for the army in France.

Among these were Northcliffe, Carson, Derby, and the King. The latter resisted every tentative effort of Lloyd George (when he became Prime Minister in December 1916) to sack Haig. A stubby figure in British Warm and riding boots, the King paid periodic visits to the front, and, while expressing suitable sentiments on the conditions in which men were forced to live in modern war, found everything mostly to his satisfaction. The Press, of course, backed the general's group almost to hysteria.

General Robertson was fifty-six years old, the son of a tailor, and had risen from the ranks. Educated at the village school, he had enlisted in the 16th Lancers at the age of seventeen. He had developed into the classical idea of the army officer of the period, but with a few remnants of his humble origins still clinging to him that many found endearing. He wined and dined well. He answered arguments with, 'I've heard different.'

Robertson saw his role as supporting Haig (known to him as "Aig") at all times against the unreliable politicians, who needed careful watching. As far as he was concerned the army was always right. Like many 'old soldiers' who owe everything to the service, he would defend it to death against the civilians. He had a deep suspicion of all foreigners. In a memo to Haig early in the year, he warned him:

> As a whole the French Commanders and Staff are a peculiar lot. Now and again in some respects they are quite good, but on some occasions they are most elemental and impracticable. The great thing to remember in dealing with them is that they are Frenchmen and not Englishmen.

Seeing his role a narrow one, Robertson did not, in fact, act as he should have done, as military adviser to the War Cabinet. He was more the agent of the army in Whitehall. This attitude did incalculable harm. It is significant that Robertson also happened to be Haig's junior in the Army List.

On 6 July after the drowning of Kitchener, Lloyd George accepted the post of Secretary of State for War. Thus a Minister was now responsible for a coming battle, which was almost impossible to stop, and in which he heartily disbelieved. But once in office, Lloyd George did nothing to try to stop it, despite his previous denunciations, and despite the fact that he had insisted on unusual powers.

Behind all was the Prime Minister himself. A white-haired Liberal, Asquith was a brilliant classical scholar from Balliol (he won a scholarship there at seventeen). He was sixty-four years of age, had been married twice, and was the centre of a devoted circle of admirers. He was acknowledged as the finest brain, the most gifted man in either House. He enjoyed mixed company; played bridge and chess. He feared God, and honoured the King. One of his sons, his eldest, was stationed at the Somme – the approaching battle of which Asquith believed might bring results. As always, his answer to critics was: 'Wait and see.'

The country waited.

CHAPTER FIVE

THE OLD FRONT LINE

THE line as it was before the Battle of the Somme came to be known as the 'Old Front Line'. It had been basically the same since 1914; during the Somme fighting men spoke of it with nostalgia. The most striking feature of the line was the large German salient, an enormous bulge into France, known as the Noyon Salient. The River Somme flowed through the northern side of this bulge. At this point of the line, by the Somme valley, there had been for two years no serious battle. On the whole, it was known as a quiet sector; there was little the French, and later the British who relieved them, could do to bother the Germans, who were in a seemingly invincible position along a long slope, and no fighting of any consequence had taken place here since the second month of the war. It never occurred to anyone that the sector would be anything else but quiet, unless the Germans themselves decided to launch a large-scale attack there.

Behind the German line the main town was Peronne; a small agricultural centre, that was now a collection of bistros surrounded by ammunition and supply dumps. The German troops spent their time unhurriedly perfecting their already excellent position. They took a pride in their shelters and trenches, and in their letters home troops boasted that their defences were the finest on the front. During the early summer of 1916 they scuttled down into their deep shelters at the first sign of a British barrage (which were infrequent), and for the rest stripped to the waist and lay down and enjoyed the sun. The gas-gongs grew rusty with disuse, and there were, it appeared, worse places to spend the war.

The main centre just behind the British line was the town of Albert. Here the streets bore signs of previous fighting and bombardments. Windows gaped vacantly into the street. Civilians carried on a make-shift life in cellars, and the famous Golden Virgin on top of the church spire leaned crazily over the square below. The church (called cathedral by the troops) was the most important building of the town. It had been built a few years previously, through the energy of a local priest, as a shrine for the Virgin of Albert. It had been thought, just before the war, that Albert might become another Lourdes. On 16 January, a Friday in 1915, just after seven a.m., a shell bent the stalk on which the gilded statue of the Virgin and Child was built. It had been suspended ever since, and it seemed to be hanging by no more than a hair. Various legends surrounded it; one was that when it fell it would mean Germany had begun the final assault that would win them the war. A French engineer kept the Virgin in place with a steel cable, just in case there was any truth in it.

Albert was a great military centre, with troops coming and going. All roads led to the front only a mile and three-quarters away. Convoys and railway columns were clattering over the cobble-stones all that May and June. The few civilians looked on without enthusiasm. It meant that a great battle was to be fought nearby. It meant more shells hurtling into the battered town. Before the war Albert had been an ugly, red-brick town where they made bicycles and sewing machines, but it had also been home.

Behind Albert was Amiens, a much larger place. Here the atmosphere was quite different. Amiens was a boom town; it had hardly ever been so gay. It was the social centre for the backdrop of the whole British sector of the line. There was a busy, active civilian life. The restaurants produced the highest cuisine for fussy British officers. The cafés and bars were crowded. Staff cars honked through the crowded streets. Men in khaki strolled on the pavements with girls by their sides. Men in wounded-blue hobbled along with newspapers giving latest news of Verdun. Aristocratic nurses flirted with officers.

Ceaselessly, guns and vans trundled through the streets out of the town and away along the great, straight, dusty, poplar-lined Route Nationale. Past an airfield, past a huge park of guns bristling like a giant porcupine, past a cavalry camp where grooms washed horses down, past ammunition dumps heavily signed with warning notices, past women working in the fields, past newly constructed railways, and on to Albert and the line.

Four roads led from Albert to the front, one of them, the state highway, was an old Roman road, one of the most important roads in France. It went towards Bapaume, behind the German line. It was one of the main avenues of the battle, and along it hundreds of thousands of men marched on their way to death.

After Albert the roads petered out into the system of trenches – with names like Centre Way, Peel Trench, Munster Alley, Dead Mule Corner, The Bowery.

Below the Somme the French held the line. North of it was British as far as Ypres and beyond. The Somme, as it meandered lazily through the line, from French and British voices to German, split up into six or seven main channels, with marshy swampland between them. It was difficult to tell which was the main channel. It was a place of small islets, buttercups, birds, and reeds. The whole thing was about five or six hundred yards across from one bank to the other.

This river had always been one of the most important military barriers of Northern France. It had been a line of defence of the Roman Empire during its decadence; traces of Roman defensive works were still to be found around its banks. It was also prominent in the Anglo-French wars.

The black muzzles of machine-guns could sometimes be discerned as the reeds waved in a gentle breeze. In the woods of Mametz and Thiepval patrols brushed through the thick undergrowth of this luxuriant, rich countryside. As fresh British troops arrived they wrote home of an air of tension at the front.

Just behind the German line there was a string of villages, on or just behind the ridge. They had names like Gommecourt, Serre, Beaumont Hamel, Pozières, Fricourt, Montauban. The villagers no longer lived there, except for a few civilian military employees, but the names would be useful before long.

CHAPTER SIX

THE PLAN

HAIG's plan was, at first, an ambitious one. The whole German trench system was to be broken along a front of many kilometres. The British forces were then to wheel outwards to the north and the French were to wheel round to the right, pushing back the exposed flanks of the enemy. A large gap was thus to be made, rather in the manner of a surgeon starting on an abdominal operation.

British and French cavalry divisions were to be sent through the gap, into the interior of the enemy's belly. The German line would then be cut in two, their armies demoralized and in confusion, and victory for the Allies as good as won. Had this plan succeeded it would not have been difficult for the German armies to withdraw behind the cut in their line, and merely reduce the size of the Noyon Salient. Also, the flanks of the intended Franco-British thrust were themselves to be exposed. The charging cavalry and the reserves, going through the gap, were to hurl themselves into a dangerous noose.

The time factor was left indefinite, although the battle was expected to be hard fought. But Haig, at least, expected the inital rupture to be made on the first day. If the plan were to succeed it was imperative that the rolling-up of the flanks started before the enemy had time to construct and organize new defences. The time factor was all-important, but only Foch of all the commanders concerned realized this fact.

Foch was, indeed, most unhappy about the whole affair. He continually told visiting dignitaries that the assault was impossible in 1916, or at any rate while the Verdun battle lasted. To break such a strong system of defences it was, he said, necessary to have a much greater concentration of attacking forces. He officially voiced his complaints before Joffre, Haig, Poincaré, and Briand. 'His excuses seemed very lame,' said Haig.

Foch's objections were overruled.

Haig's whole plan depended on one factor. It depended on the success of his initial artillery bombardment, by means of which he hoped so to destroy the enemy's first system that the advancing infantry would be able to make their great blow at almost full force and power.

There seems no doubt that Haig really hoped to lead a British Army to decisive victory on the Somme. At the same time he knew that if it did not come off he would always be able to carry on the battle of attrition that Joffre wished for.

The main burden of the British attack was to be entrusted to General Rawlinson and his new Fourth Army, which consisted mostly of volunteer Kitchener soldiers or Territorial Army units. Allenby's Third Army, to the north, was to make a subsidiary attack near Gommecourt. Haig was now assembling a great mass of troops to follow up the attack, remembering that failure at Loos was partly due to support not being sent forward quickly enough (the failure at Loos, for which he blamed Sir John French, always rankled with Haig). And remembering that failure at Neuve Chapelle was because the break in the enemy line was too narrow, he decided to attack on at least an eighteen-mile front.

Although he had originally wanted his attack in Flanders and later in the year, Haig, overruled by Joffre, was now giving every bit of grit and stubbornness he possessed, which was considerable, to organizing the preparations for the great battle. He forgot his previous preference and entered into the plans and arrangements wholeheartedly.

He wanted the first wave to go over the top at first light, in the gloom, because of the German machine-gunners. But Joffre and Foch preferred a later time so that their artillery observers would be able to see the progress of their troops.

As the weeks went on and it became plain that the French share of the battle was to be much smaller than originally planned, the major reason for the choice of the Somme area by Joffre (that he liked the idea of the French and British making a combined attack, side by side) was less important, but no one thought of changing the field of intended operations to a more suitable and promising place. By now it was too late. Preparations were under way, and enormous supplies and stocks were piling up behind the line.

It had always been Joffre's intention, from the original plan in the winter, that Haig should keep harassing the German line on the Somme before the main assault with minor attacks. 'Winter sports', Haig jocularly called this idea (about the only attempt at humour in his published diaries, it is in sad taste).

36

One way and another, Haig managed to escape from this commitment.

The Third Army, under Allenby, was moved before the attack to between the Ancre and Arras to make way for Rawlinson's Fourth Army. Although a part of his force, two divisions, were to make a subsidiary attack on the left flank of Rawlinson, Allenby was seldom brought into the councils of Haig. He made it clear that he 'did not approve' of the plan, however, and suggested a more effective and less costly subsidiary attack farther north. It was turned down.

Allenby and Haig had known each other for years. They had always been rivals and still were. If there was anyone Haig disliked more than Sir John French, it was General Sir Edmund Allenby. They had been to Staff College together in 1896, and Allenby had been made master of drag hounds there in preference to Haig, who was, in fact, a better horseman. Allenby, a heavy, awkward man, looking like a human caricature of a traditional soldier, was always uncomfortable in Haig's presence. He would normally stop talking at the appearance of Haig within earshot and would fidget and cough until he was separated from the confident, trim Scotsman. Allenby was known as 'Bull', Haig as 'Lucky'.

Allenby had finished the South African War as a Lieutenant-Colonel in the 5th Lancers. But in competition with Haig (they were born the same year), he had lost ground, despite the fact that Allenby had been the more successful of the two as a leader. Haig was a *full* Colonel soon after the end of the same war and he was mixing with royalty, two facts that made all the difference. Although Haig had been commissioned three years later than Allenby, by 1903 he had overtaken him. Less than two years after the South African War, Haig was a Major-General. The difference of recognition in South Africa of these two men was to have a real effect on the course of the World War. Not till five years after Haig was Allenby made a Major-General. Throughout the first half of the war on the Western Front there was this thick-set, bullish man, always at Haig's shoulder. Several times he might have replaced him. But Haig was saved by the influence of the King, and by Asquith's indecision.

There were not many in 1916 who were able to tell correctly which was the military genius and which was not; the self-assured, sprightly Haig, or the slow-moving, inarticulate Allenby.

General Rawlinson, however, was more happy under Haig's command. A product of Eton, Sandhurst, and India, he had few deviations from the conventional British officer of the period. One of them was that he had had experience of guerilla warfare in Burma, but this, alas, did not apparently have the effect on his ideas on modern warfare that it might have done. Another deviation was that he was not a cavalryman – one of the very few generals who were not. He was, on the other hand, from the Guards, which, if one could not get into a top cavalry regiment, was the next best thing. Like many of his contemporaries, he had been blooded at Omdurman. He had immense experience of staff work, in which he had distinguished himself in South Africa. And before the war he had been Commandant of the Staff College. He was greatly respected and liked by all his contemporaries. He was, surprisingly, a personal friend of Winston Churchill's of many years' standing.

Sir Henry Rawlinson was probably the finest polo player of all the generals on the Western Front, which meant that he was possibly the finest polo player in the army. He influenced the game both in India and at home.

Despite his conventional background, unlike some other officers, Rawlinson was not above doing a little thinking for himself. He was even capable of questioning orders. He distrusted Haig's plan for the Somme. He believed that there should be a series of limited attacks with modest objectives; unlike Haig, who seemed to persist in visions of victory in one mighty blow.

On 19 April 'Rawly' sent a memorandum to G.H.Q. outlining his thoughts on the coming offensive. He said he saw two possible courses of attack. The first was to capture all of the German defensive system in one go (this was Haig's idea). The second was to attack in two phases, each phase having a limited objective.

There were, he said, considerable risks in the first choice. He outlined seven objections to it.

(1) The longish distance which would have to be covered by British infantry between the German first and second lines.

(2) The strength of Pozières and Contalmaison, which he referred to as 'fortified villages'.

(3) The strength of the German second line, which had support as well as front trenches and was well wired throughout.

38

(4) The difficulty of cutting the wire in front of this line.

(5) The probability of German reserves reaching the second line before his troops could.

(6) The difficulty of supporting his infantry with artillery fire should they get to the German second line.

(7) The fact that most of his troops were new; too new to undertake such a formidable and difficult attack.

Rawlinson had quite a row with his chief about this, but in the end he gave way – as he had to. Having given his opinion, he got down wholeheartedly to preparing for something in which he had no confidence. This attitude was the very spirit of the European armies.

On 30 April Rawlinson wrote: 'I still think we could do better to proceed by shorter steps; but I have told D.H. I will carry out his plan with as much enthusiasm as if it were my own.'

'But privately,' says the *Official History of the War*, 'he was convinced that they [Haig's plans] were based on false premises, and too great optimism, for there was no sign that German morale was weakening, and until that happened anything in the nature of a decisive success was out of the question.'

Haig had disliked Joffre's decision to attack at the Somme. Now he was, in his turn, bullying his senior commanders into accepting a plan in which they had no confidence. He was full of the scent of battle. And soon Rawlinson, too, was to be sniffing out the disbelievers among his officers. And in the end, when Haig's plan failed, he got his way after all.

Commanding officers were always right. They had to be; it was the only way the army would work.

Well, there it was. The Fourth Army, under Rawlinson, with a little diversionary help from Allenby's Third, was to attack in the last week of June. A great gap was to be pushed through the German line. The British were to 'roll' that line away northwards and eastwards. Lieutenant-General Sir Hubert Gough, all memory of the 'mutiny' at the Curragh forgotten and forgiven, was to charge through the gap with three cavalry divisions. It was an exciting project. Joffre was well pleased; especially as he was certain that attrition would result.

With all this settled, Haig left for London on Tuesday, 6 June. He left by the mail boat at one fifteen from Boulogne (the kind of fact which he always carefully recorded in his diary.) At Dover he was shown a telegram from the police by the Military Landing Officer. It reported that Lord Kitchener and his staff had been drowned in the sinking of H.M.S. *Hampshire*. Kitchener had always been one of Haig's mentors. On Haig's appointment as C-in-C in France, he had sent him a touching and sincere message.

Douglas Haig only found nine words to record this event, which shook Europe, in his diary: 'Ship struck a mine and sank. Sea very rough.' Here, indeed, was a revealing insensitivity to loss of life.

The following day he met the War Council at 10 Downing Street ('at 11.30'). Haig wrote:

> At the end of the Meeting the Prime Minster said the Government had complete confidence in me, but would like to ask me a few questions. These resolved themselves into the question about the Ypres Salient, and another about the nature of the recent fighting. I easily satisfied them as to why it was necessary to hold on to the salient and the causes of the casualties amongst the Canadians. Incidentally, I reproved Bonar Law for listening to some pluckless Canadians who had urged on him the abandonment of the Ypres salient.

Afterwards, Haig lunched with his wife Doris at their flat ('at 1.30') and then they went to the Alhambra to see the 'Bing Bong Brothers' [*sic*]. He enjoyed the show, but had to leave early. At five forty-five he went to Buckingham Palace, where he saw his friend the King. They talked for an hour and a quarter.

> He thought the Cavalry should be reduced on account of the cost of maintenance. We could carry on the war for a very long time provided the cost did not exceed £5,000,000 a day. I protested that it would be unwise, because in order to shorten the war, and reap the fruits of any success, we must make use of the mobility of the Cavalry.

> On 9 June, a French delegation with Briand, the Prime

Minister, and Joffre, came to London. They met the British War Committee and Haig at Downing Street, and pressed not only for the Somme offensive but for a continuation and extension of the Salonika campaign.

After the conference with the French, Haig supplied Asquith with some notes on the coming offensive.

It is to be a battle of *durée prolongée* and Joffre had urged me to be ready to carry out frequent reliefs of the divisions engaged. Sound policy, therefore, required that all our resources in men and ammunition should be sent to the decisive points, viz: France and not wasted against the Bulgars in the Balkans, or any other secondary objective.

Haig went off to Deal, where he spent a few days playing golf with his wife before returning to France.

There is a vagueness about Haig's plan at this point. On one day he is speaking of a violent break-through and spectacular cavalry charges. On the next of a so-called 'battle of *durée prolongée*'.

On 30 June Charteris wrote in his diary:

We do not expect any great advance, or any great place or arms to fall to us now. We are fighting primarily to wear down the German armies and the German nation. The casualty list will be big.

How does this attitude of his staff fit in with Haig's own starry visions, to say nothing of his large force of cavalry? On 16 June Haig wrote:

The advance is to be pressed eastwards far enough to enable our cavalry to push through into the open country beyond the enemy's prepared lines of defence.

On 28 June, after receiving a memorandum from Foch, Haig wrote of objectives as ambitious as these:

[I received] an unsigned letter from Foch criticizing my plan of first enlarging the gap made towards Arras, and suggesting that British should first of all extend their right to Sailly-Saillisel so as to enable the French to get forward. I did not reply to the document. ... At 5 p.m. I met Joffre ... he raised the same points as Foch had outlined in his note. I pointed out that if I did not at once take the offensive northwards as soon as Bapaume was occupied by us, the enemy would be sure to attack us from the north and cut us from our base. The old man looked tired and rubbed his head. He evidently saw the force of my argument but Foch had got at him.

In fact Bapaume was still unoccupied five months later, although it was only eight miles from the British front on 1

July. A gap towards Arras was never even thought about after the first days of the battle. Foch might well have been a little bewildered. He need not have had any fears, however, that the French part of the assault would get left behind.

Even if he was a little dilatory about his objectives, Haig was nothing if not confident. He had reason to be. He wrote: 'I feel that every step in my plan has been taken with the Divine help.'

CHAPTER SEVEN

PREPARATIONS

MOST of the great army now being prepared for the Somme offensive had never before been farther from home than Southend. And most of its soldiers had never been expected to don a military uniform in their lives; that was left to professional soldiers, about whom they read with awe in the *Bystander* and the newspapers. And yet, here they were, volunteering in their thousands, giving up homes and wives and parents, and comfortable existences, for the uncertainties of France and Flanders. But rumours of disasters and disullusion were still only rumours at the beginning of 1916. No one took them too seriously. The Boche were taking a little longer to beat than it had at first been thought. They were proving a tough nut to crack. But they had to be beaten before long, although nobody quite knew why.

Kitchener got his enormous army of volunteers, a quite unprecedented feat in British history, from some of the least war-like people in Europe. From people who had never seen a soldier in uniform, from crofters in Cumberland, from fishermen in Wick, from shopkeepers in Leeds, from dancing instructors in Fulham. From men who had always thought really large battles, the kind in which white men faced white, were peculiarly continental pastimes, like naked women in magazines and emperors being assassinated.

They came to a strange military life because their King and country needed them, because their friends were going, because it was generally accepted to be cowardly not to, because they had visions of tattoo-like pageantry, because they were suffused with patriotism of the noblest kind, and because the Hun had to be taught a lesson and, by jingo, it was high time too.

How were these new armies to be used? This was a real problem because the Germans were still able to field a vast experienced army of well-trained soldiers, which logically should have been able to deal with the British amateurs without much difficulty.

Kitchener wished them to be used as a whole. He envisaged

whole armies of shopkeepers gloriously marching to the Rhine. Sir John French, however, wished them to be integrated, probably at battalion strength, with the regular troops. French's view was supported by Churchill, at that time First Lord of the Admiralty. Churchill sent a memorandum to Asquith on 6 January 1915.

I think there is a great deal to be said for the principle which Sir John French advocates, of intermingling units from the new armies with those of the regular forces now serving in the field. It is undesirable that British armies serving side by side in one theatre of the war should show great differences in character, experience and training; and that the British line should be maintained at one point over a very large front by army corps which have seen all the hardest fighting, while another equally large section of the front line is to be held by an army or armies who come entirely new to active service, whose training, though excellent, has been very short. Such a system ... would certainly not give the new troops the best chance of distinguishing themselves.

But Sir John French was recalled and Winston Churchill was disgraced. And by the time Lord Kitchener sank into the stormy waves of the North Sea he had mostly got his way. A great new army was in France; an army of untried civilians. It was a monument to his industry, his foresight, and his confidence. Whether the composition of the Fourth Army greatly affected the coming tragedy is unlikely, but at least an army more on the lines suggested by French and Churchill would have stood a better chance.

Haig was not greatly perturbed by this question, one way or the other; all he wanted was men. If his plans succeeded then there would be a great victory for any army. If they did not, then it did not greatly matter what kind of soldiers they were, so long as they could stay alive in a trench and operate a howitzer.

Because the Old Army had been hard-pressed all the war, it had been able to spare but few instructors to train the New Armies. Not untill they got to France did the recruits receive training, making use of the latest experiences of trench warfare. And even this training was quite inadequate and overoptimistic. At the camps at home, the instructors were a few officers on leave from the Indian Army, retired officers (some

44

wore Crimea ribbons), ex-N.C.O.s, and men who had hardly left the regimental depots in their entire army careers. Few of them had any ideas as to what this new kind of war was really like. And many of the men left for France as innocent of modern warfare as when they had joined up.

Various tricks were used to raise regiments. There were trades' regiments, there were regiments for professions (lawyers, civil servants, artists). Officers were in great shortage, as they had an almost inescapable mortality in the line. French had written: 'I was really, positively, at my wits end, suffering almost agony, to know where I could get reinforcements.'

At first, training consisted of only six weeks for officers (including forty-eight hours in the line), then of three months. Either way it was not very much. Training at home for the rank and file of K's new army usually lasted up to ten months. Most of those who went through it later considered it a waste of time. With instructors ignorant of real conditions and needs, bound to some textbooks that had applied to the Zulu Wars, it was mostly irrelevant.

Alex Potter, in an East Anglian battalion, wrote in a series of articles *Memories of a Kitchener's Man* in the *Continental Daily Mail* in November 1939:

> A few lessons on how to dig and drain trenches, on raiding, fixing up barbed wire, using Very lights, caring for trench feet, using a machine-gun, dodging mortar bombs, and helping sappers at mining wouldn't have been amiss.
>
> Drilling, marching, musketry, physical jerks, advancing in artillery formation, and a few other open warfare manoeuvres about made up our training. Looking back on that training period I remember chiefly the rich comradeship it brought; a new-found pride in the county that gave our battalion its name; our amazing vitality, and the certainty that I was going to die. In the pubs at night we saw some of the Regular Army boys, back wounded from France and Belguim. We wondered why they didn't talk much about what they had seen.

As the new officers came streaming in, there was a wave of astonishment among the survivors of the old regulars. Here were men who had never sat in a saddle (except that of a bicycle), who had never swung from the chandeliers (and were not ashamed of it); who had never given orders to servants (and looked uncomfortable doing it now); here were men who actually sat about and read. And here they were in the regimental mess.

It was these new young officers, and the soldiers they commanded, who brought completely new notions to army life. Never before, for instance, had the mistrust of 'red tabs', the staff officers well behind the line and mostly out of danger, been so strong. Here were men who, after only a few months, actually questioned the system; suggested it might not always be perfect. But on the whole it was generally agreed that they were making surprisingly good soldiers and putting up a good show – even if most of them were not gentlemen and many of them would never really understand the meaning of the word 'discipline'.

By 1 July Rawlinson's army consisted of 511,676 men, of whom about a hundred thousand were to go over the top in the first assault. All the military experts in Europe were waiting to see whether this new amateur army, raised, trained, and equipped in less than two years, with no tradition to uphold, was a match for the Kaiser's military machine.

For many, generals and privates, cooks and doctors, the journey started at Victoria or Charing Cross stations; places in London to which the Western Front could stretch an atmospheric tentacle. Wives smiled bravely, children wept, departing soldiers were tight-lipped and silent, others waved and shouted. As the train pulled out great cheers went up and the tightly packed crowds swayed and pressed forward.

Suddenly, the train was out of the station, before the things which should have been said ever were said. Little suburban villas slipped past the windows, men lit cigarettes and mopped their brows – it was a hot summer. Past the fruit trees of Kent, puffing away through the countryside of England; Scotsmen gazed at the south for the first time in their lives. They played cards, and they talked of the girls they had left behind. They hummed the top songs of the moment. No one could deny that it was all exciting. Off at last.

The vast majority of troops crossed from Folkestone to Boulogne. Many of them fainted on the way from overheating, due to the tightly fitting, much-advertised 'body-shields' that were meant to stop bullets at all but the closest range. Other arteries were Southampton-Havre, for heavy baggage and stores; and Dover-Calais, for heavy ammunition and stores.

By mid-1916, Boulogne had become a largely British administered city. With its rest camps, its hospitals and offices and clerks working in the base, there was a large British population. You could get fried fish and chips as easily as at home. You could not visit a bar without hearing an English voice.

After disembarking, the troops marched through the cobbled streets. Sometimes they were singing:

> Here we are,
> Here we are,
> Here we are again.

It sounded gay enough, but a few observers were disturbed to feel a fatalistic ring in the words.

The main base was at Étaples, outside Boulogne, in a country of sand-dunes, tufts of grass, and continual sea winds. Most of the reinforcements were sent to the base here, before setting out for the front. A huge city of huts and tents had been built. As they got off the train at Étaples, new arrivals were astonished at the size of this camp, or, rather, system of camps. It seemed to stretch away right across northern France.

Here they first met with the 'base-wallah Huns'. These men, officer clerks, always seemed to get everything wrong, to bungle the simplest problems of demand and supply. Officers were likely to be posted to any regiment. Black Watch were issued with trews for going to the Devons, while in the next camp an equal number of Dorsets were issued with kilts for going to the Black Watch. Naturally, this kind of thing caused a good deal of frustration and discontent.

At Étaples was the famous 'Bull Ring', an enormous training ground. Here the new soldiers were put through their paces for the first time by men who had had long experience of the front. And not far away was the resort of Paris Plage, with its long, deserted promenade, its shuttered windows and its air of 'closed-up-for-the-duration'. While they waited to go to the line, on an evening off, some took the steam train to Paris Plage, but it usually seemed a wasted trip.

Then, one day, began the crowded train journey and the long march to Albert and the Western Front.

Everyone who went on this march, and half a million did, although not so many returned, and has recorded it, remembers it as a deep experience. The countryside was particularly beautiful. Birds twittered overhead, the sun beat down on all below, and the harvest was clearly going to be an exceptional one. On their way to a mystery, to something that might turn out to be a land of horror, men are inclined to notice such things – things they would normally pass by.

Drums beat, steadily tapping out the time. Boots clapped in unison on the dusty roads; the columns halted for ten minutes in every hour.

Henry Williamson wrote:

The wind waves of summer were upon the barleys, the wheat was upright and rustling, the oats shook their green sprays. Old men with scythes were cutting hay to the tramp – tramp – tramp of nailed boots between the ever-widening rows of poplars shaking all their leaves like little heliographs or as though waving goodbye. They marched through villages of lime-washed *pisée* and thatch, where children stood and stared, but waved no more; for hundreds of thousands of *les Anglais* had already passed that way, singing, whistling, and shouting the same remarks.

Yes, they sang as they marched through the beauties of a French summer. They sang:

> There's a long, long trail a-winding,
> Into the land of my dreams,
> Where the nightingale is singing
> And a pale moon beams.

An anonymous soldier described the scene in his diary:

The sky is flecked with white clouds whose shadows chase across the undulating, wooded country. The tall corn is ripening, and between its stalks poppies and cornflowers glow with colour. Through the valley we are descending, a rising stream finds its way, and on the hills beyond, great elm trees stand like wise men brooding. It is a lush, green country, full of beauty. The war seems far away.

Thousands and thousands tramped on to take up their positions for the battle. Engineers and engine-drivers, shepherds and accountants, tinkers and tailors, butchers and bakers. Things, they thought, couldn't be *too* bad at the front.

> A German officer crossed the Rhine,
> Parlez-vous,
> A German officer crossed the Rhine,
> Out to get him some women and wine,
> Inky-pinky parlez-vous.

Oh, landlord where is your daughter fair?
Skiboo! Skiboo!
Oh, landlord where is your daughter fair
With lily-white tits and golden hair...?

The songs drifted away across the golden fields and the cool shady woods, until they were nothing but a distant, meaningless murmur.

In the camps and villages around Albert, now a huge military zone, the new battalions waited for the day not yet announced. Everyone knew the 'Big Push' was going to start almost any day; it must be very soon now. They settled in as best they could in the little cottage billets, in the barns, and under canvas. They began to get that feel of the front that those who were there have found so difficult to convey to those who were not.

They spoke of Blighty, and heard old soldiers (of a few months) talk of 'Blighty' wounds. They ate bread and pozzy (jam), and drank mugs of char. They smoked Woods and ate Bombadier Fritz (*pommes de terre frites*) at the local cafés.

They wore the new tin helmets that to many seemed to give, at first, a ludicrous Chinese effect. On pay-days a private was handed a pale-blue five-franc note (worth about four shillings). But their needs were few, and they saved the rest of their pay (varying from a shilling a day to six and sixpence), less stoppages, for the leave they hoped to be getting when the 'Show' was over.

On joining their units (those who arrived in small groups), they met with conflicting welcomes, depending on the unit concerned, and how long it had been at the front. In some, full chamber-pots lay around in officers' quarters, uniforms were despised as like those of 'base-wallahs' if they did not show obvious signs of wear and battle, and officers reeked of whisky. 'This war will be won on whisky, or it won't be won at all,' as one of them said.

Those were units that had been in the line for a month or two, and had already had considerable experience of raids. Officers often seemed to be young boys. Many of them were acting majors, or even senior, in their early twenties. Some had prematurely grey hair.

In other units discipline and custom (kept on by the handful of regular officers) were severe. Field punishment was still in use, and there was nothing unusual in seeing a boy strapped to the wheel of a field kitchen. That was Field Punishment No. 1. Other penalties were doing pack-drill under provost-sergeants, and latrine duties. Volunteers suddenly discovered, with an uncomfortable shock, that this war was different from the one they had read about in the newspapers.

And they waited.

They learnt all about 'Maconochie' (a tin of meat and vegetables). They began to diet on bully-beef, large thick biscuits, apple jam, slabs of cheese, plum jam, strong tea with condensed milk, and tinned, evil-tasting butter. During quiet periods there was bacon for breakfast, and stew at midday.

They went to the forward trenches for a tour of duty, to raise the parapets (especially at night) and to carry out raids. The first time in the trenches, with the Germans somewhere across there on that slope, over the grass, was an unforgettable experience for the fresh soldier.

Robert Graves has written:

> The familiar trench smell of 1915-17 still haunts my nostrils: compounded of stagnant mud, latrine buckets, chloride of lime, unburied or half-buried corpses, rotting sandbags, stale human sweat, fumes of cordite and lyddite. Sometimes it was sweetened by cigarette smoke and the scent of bacon frying over wood fires (broken ammunition boxes); sometimes made sinister by the lingering odour of poison gas.

There was plenty of activity on the Somme before the battle. The enemy continually sent over canisters; says Graves

> a two-gallon drum with a cylinder inside containing almost two pounds of an explosive called ammonal that looked like salmon paste, smelled like marzipan and, when it went off, sounded like the Day of Judgement. The hollow around the cylinder contained scrap metal, apparently collected by French villagers behind the German lines: rusty nails, fragments of British and French shells, spent bullets, and the screws, nuts and bolts that the heavy lorries leave behind on the road. We dissected one unexploded canister and found in it, among other things, the cog-wheels of a clock, and half a set of false teeth.

How the canister was fired remained a mystery until 1 July, when a wooden cannon was found. Its crew offered to surrender, but their fate had been sealed months before by impatient, frustrated British soldiers.

Casualties were steady throughout May and June as the Fourth Army expanded, like a greedy belly, and as the men waited. In a typical platoon of fifty, twelve were killed or wounded in the year before the Somme, not more than three of the platoon seeing a German in all that time.

Says Graves:

> We busied ourselves raising the front-line parapet and building traverses to limit the damage of the trench-mortar shells that fell continually. Every night not only the companies in the front line, but both support companies kept hard at work all the time. It was an even worse place than Guinchy for rats; they scuttled about A Company mess at mealtimes. We always ate with revolvers beside our plates, and punctuated our conversation with sudden volleys at a rat rummaging at somebody's valise or crawling along the timber support of the roof above our heads.

> Western Front rats, feeding on the flesh of corpses, were becoming giant-sized. (T. B. 'Tubby' Clayton, once saw one at Ypres that 'measured about 4ft. from stem to stern'.) Alex Potter, in the Somme trenches before the battle, saw 'a rat bite a sergeant's ear while he snored. I woke with one on my face. They got used to the troops. I saw one, instead of running away, just walking off.' Boots had to be worn at night and faces covered; food suspended in bags from dug-out ceilings.

Meanwhile, behind the line, training went on for the battle. Monchy-Breton ('Monkey-Britain') was the most favoured place, as the ground there was something like that of the coming battlefield. Full-scale practices were carried out. The Albert-Bapaume road, which ran through the real battlefield, was marked out with ribbons. Distances and timings were carefully observed. Young staff officers ran around blowing whistles and making notes on paper clipped to boards. Gas was loosed over 'attacking' troops, blanks were fired, wire was run out at the edge of swiftly 'captured' woods. And, wrote Edmund Blunden, bayonet drill was given by 'well-fed, wool-clad gymnastic instructors'.

Bayonet drill became a kind of fetish before the Somme. In the minds of staff officers it seems to have become a panacea for their doubts as to the coming offensive. There was going to be an infantry charge. These amateur soldiers must get used to the idea of cold steel.

Wrote 'Mark VII' (pseudonym of Mark Plowman):

> Why, indeed, should we spare a fat German just because he throws up his hands and shouts 'Kamarad', when, as the lecturer says, if we let him live, he may become the father of ten more Huns? Killing is the job for infantrymen, and if we don't like killing, why did we join the infantry? The bayonet is the logical conclusion of all fighting; there you get to the real thing. But we must not overdo it. Three inches is enough. Don't go and bury the muzzle of your rifle in your man and then find you can't get your bayonet out no matter how you stamp on him.

The Fourth Army School was at Flixécourt, a small town not far from Amiens. Here officers and N.C.O.s were sent on short courses. Time was divided between parades, lectures, and practices. Tactics were taught by instructors who said that they were in favour of open warfare, which was, they said, bound to come soon. The young officers moved troops about with pencils on pieces of paper.

Famous big-game hunters gave lectures on sniping (rifles were seldom used in the trenches, except as clubs). The Commandant of the school had a motto: 'Always do your utmost.' And a Highland Major lectured on the 'Spirit of the Bayonet'.

Blunden and Plowman were by no means the only young poets preparing for battle in the summer of 1916. Siegfried Sassoon was at the School at Flixécourt, and has described the bayonet lessons that became so much a part of life, part hysterical, part fearful, before the Somme.

> He [the Major] spoke with homicidal eloquence, keeping the game alive with genial and well-judged jokes. Man, it seemed, had been created to jab the life out of the Germans. To hear the Major talk one might have thought that he did it himself every day before breakfast. His final words were: 'Remember that every Boche you fellows kill is a point scored to our side; every Boche you kill brings victory one minute nearer. Kill them! Kill them!'

If this was not clear enough, there was always the *Manual of Bayonet Training*.

> To attack with the bayonet effectively requires Good Dir-

ection, Strength and Quickness, during a state of wild excitement and probably physical exhaustion. In a bayonet assault all ranks go forward to kill or be killed and only those who have developed skill and strength by constant training will be able to kill.

The Highland Major was awarded the D.S.O. for his lecturing.

Among the instructors was a Major Archibald Wavell. He helped to introduce a new weapon, called the Lewis Gun. He described it as a haphazard, hand to mouth affair.

He was also put in charge of encouraging volunteers for balloon duties. Captive balloons were to be tethered close behind the line, and observers in them would report on enemy batteries and movements. Wavell had no idea what it would be like in a balloon (he had already been half-blinded at Ypres), but he sold the idea well. He described the beauties of 'getting away from it all up in the clouds'. Actually, the job turned out to be highly dangerous, many of the balloons coming loose. (The Buckingham Bullet was used by the British the day before the Somme started. It was a surprise, and consequently a success. Fired from an aircraft, it set enemy balloons on fire. The German observers had to jump with recently invented parachutes.)

Major Wavell (later Field-Marshal Lord Wavell) was not the only future military genius quietly assessing for himself the standard of generalship in 1916. There was also a Major Montgomery on the Somme.

One of the many things they must have pondered on was the usefulness of raids in which large parties of men were sent over the top, merely, it sometimes seemed, to keep the line in action.

It was generally thought by all concerned, except by the staff officers who planned or ordered them, that raids were a useless loss of life. They discouraged those taking part and their objects seemed trivial compared with the casualties which were almost invariably their result.

Known as 'flying matinées', each division was expected to provide one at fairly frequent intervals. At least one division asked its battalions to put forward a scheme for a raid. The one with the best scheme would carry it out. There was little enthusiasm. This serves to show, as well as anything, how out of touch divisional staffs were with the attitude of the infantry. But 'Papa' Joffre had to be pleased, and he required activity on the front.

A great deal of information was admittedly collected in this way, but how much it was to effect the tactical approach of the general staff is doubtful. Names of regiments of the German troops in the line were particularly sought after, for some reason. But no one seems to have asked raiding parties or prisoners about the depth of German dug-outs.

Raiding parties were led up to the front trenches by torch, often a hundred or more strong; sometimes of only half a dozen. Their faces blackened with burnt cork, they cracked jokes, and prepared as if for a minstrel show at a concert party. With Mills bombs and hatchets they crept over the parapets, after a liberal issue of rum, and crawled through previously cut gaps in the British wire.

As the flares and gun flashes lit up the night sky of the battlefield, they scuttled from crater to crater; whispering, cursing, splashing in water. The clinking and creaking of their own equipment and the pounding of their hearts mingled with the dull, heavy explosions farther down the line. They were usually spotted and were subjected to German mortar fire, hurrying back as best they could to their own trenches, carrying their wounded, to be congratulated on a 'good show'. Such information as they brought back was often compounded of unreliable guess-work or useless, well-known details.

Apart from raids and training, there was much administrative preparation to be done. This administrative detail, indeed, helped to fix the date of the battle. Haig himself was not satisfied that his vast military machine would be well-oiled and thoroughly prepared for the task ahead by 1 July.

The district consisted of simple agricultural land and there were, at first, no facilities for harbouring half a million men and a hundred thousand horses. Railways had to be built, both standard and narrow gauges. Vast stocks of ammunition and stores of all kinds had to be brought up to behind the line. From 8 June seven ammunition trains arrived each day; after 15 June they were increased to ten a day. Tramways were constructed. Available roads were improved, new ones built. Causeways were made over marshy valleys. Miles and miles of deep communication trench had laboriously to be dug – to say nothing of trenches for telephone wires, assault and assembly trenches, gun emplacements and observation posts.

Accommodation in the villages was not nearly adequate. A great, temporary city had to be improvised. Little water was available apart from the village wells and that of the Somme itself. A hundred and twenty miles of water pipe had to be laid down. (Instructions read: 'Washing must be reduced to a minimum.') Timber for bridges had to be brought up, and road metal, and cables.

Bomb-proof shelters and hospitals had to be constructed. Prisoners' cages had to be prepared (this for the first time by the British on the Western Front). Aerial photography had to be carried out. New gas masks were issued – known in Robert Graves's unit as 'the goggle-eyed booger with the tit'.

The British went about all these preparations with an incredibly careless indifference to what their foes could see. This casualness had already cost them dearly in the war, but seems to have made no difference. Almost the only covering measure the British took was to spread rumours that the coming attack was to be farther north. While it was believed by British intelligence that their ruse had taken in the Germans, the German High Command was busily sending reinforcements to the Somme.

On 17 May Rawlinson issued a thirty-one-page pamphlet, *Tactical Notes,* to be issued down to captains (his staff had to do it themselves, as G.H.Q., whose job it was, had no time for it). The booklet described the correct method of infantry advance, as it would a movement on the parade ground: 'The leading lines should not be more than 100 yards apart, with the men in each line extended at two or three paces interval.'

There was no mention of rifle or machine-gun covering fire, or of the possibilities of night or dawn attacks, or of the necessity of crossing No Man's Land at speed so as to reach the trenches opposite before the enemy had time to recover from the barrage. There was no suggestion that where opposition was strong, attacks were to be halted and reinforcements sent to where it was weak and where a break-through was a possibility. No allowance was made for any flexibility of the steady advance of the various waves. But one thing *was* made clear: 'All must be prepared for heavy casualties.'

The Royal Flying Corps, an already legendary, highly publicized body of men, was preparing in the battle area too. It had gained something near to complete mastery in the air in this region, although the occasional German plane was still able to fly over for observation purposes, and even for strafing (although this had not come into general use) and continued to do so throughout the battle. The Air Commander, Major-General H. M. Trenchard, had 185 aircraft. The Germans had 129, but some of these were needed south of the Somme against the French. On the first day of battle there were only nine combats in the air, and the British preparations were never severely interfered with from above, although no doubt they were fully observed. The R.F.C. carried out reconnaissance, photography, spotting for the artillery, and bombing (three railway stations were bombed on 1 July). One of the pilots later became Lord Dowding, chief of Fighter Command during the Battle of Britain.

Throughout the days before the battle commenced, planes hovered and buzzed about in the blue summer skies; D.H. 2s, Nieuports, Sopwith 2-seaters, F.E. 2bs, and B.E.s. Troops gazed up, wondering at the tiny machines. A rumour was passed round that the Kaiser had offered to surrender and that the R.F.C. were providing an escort to the delegation which were going to discuss terms.

Below the ground as well as over it, men were busily preparing for the Push.

Deep, long mines were being constructed, as near to the enemy line as possible, to be blown up near zero hour. Men worked in bare feet, stripped to the waist in primitive conditions. Sweat pouring off them, little miners from Durham and South Wales worked as they had never done before. Everything was done in complete silence. Listeners, at listening posts, waited for a muffled cough or a laugh to tell that they were getting dangerously close to enemy dug-outs or countermines.

Eight large mines and eleven small ones were dug. The mine at La Boisselle was one of the most enormous of the war. It left a crater 320 yards round at the top. Sir William Orpen, the artist, saw it in 1917; a huge hill of white chalk, thrown up from below, surrounded it like a lip. The sides were so steep that steps had had to be cut down it. Far down there was a small mound, with a skull placed on top. Around were the remains of humanity that had been there. But in June 1916, that German humanity knew nothing of the little British miners, or of what they were so busily working for.

According to the *Official History of the War*:

On the first day of the Somme, though many mines were fired, they were too much scattered up and down the front to produce a noticeable effect on the enemy; and the firing of one mine ten minutes before zero, by higher order, gave the enemy warning of the coming assault.

Tunnels were also built to near the German lines, so that men would be able to advance under cover. This mining and tunnelling was one of the few skilful aspects of the Battle of the Somme. All kinds of methods were used to avoid being overheard. Vinegar was poured into holes at the face, thus softening the chalk, which was then scooped out. Gallery floors were carpeted with sandbags. As one man caught dislodged bits of chalk, another scooped with a bayonet. Mine tunnels were about four and a half feet by two and a half, and an advance of eighteen inches in twenty four hours was considered good going. Men sitting on the floor passed back the waste. The longest tunnel was 1,030 feet long. Communication tunnels were higher, about eight and a half feet, and were about fourteen feet below ground. One engineer actually penetrated a German dug-out by mistake and withdrew unnoticed.

There were a hundred and one other preparations that needed attending to before a battle like the Somme, the largest that a British army had ever undertaken, could be fought. Water and ration parties had to be detailed and instructed. Equipment had to be checked. Maps had to be examined. N.C.O.s had to be informed. Signallers and runners had to have their roles carefully explained to them.

Times of artillery lifts, signals of Very light and rocket, code words of companies and neighbouring units – all had to be learned by heart. Fatigue parties for carrying shells, working parties for carrying barbed wire, any kind of parties for digging and sandbagging and roofing – all had to be organized.

Each battalion had to be supplied with its pigeon officer (part-time). During the battle birds were to be kept in Corps Mobile lofts; old London omnibuses. Volunteers were not easy to find; pigeon officers were considered a thorough nuisance.

Lord Montgomery remembered the following story:

During the Somme battle an infantry brigade which had better remain nameless was to be the leading brigade in a divisional attack. It was important that the Brigade Commander should receive early information of the progress of his forward troops, and intense interest was aroused when it was disclosed that a pigeon would be used to carry the news.

When the day of the attack arrived the pigeon was given to a soldier to carry. He was to go with the leading sub-units and was told that at a certain moment an officer would write a message to be fastened to the pigeon's leg; he would then release the pigeon which would fly back to its loft at Brigade H.Q.

Time slipped by, but no pigeon arrived – the Brigadier walked feverishly about outside his dug-out. The soldiers anxiously searched the skies – there was no sign of any pigeon. At last the cry went up: 'The pigeon!' And sure enough it alighted safely in the loft.

Soldiers rushed to get the news and the Brigadier Commander roared out: 'Give me the message!'

It was handed to him and this is what he read: 'I am absolutely fed up with carrying this bloody bird about France.'

Birds, men, machines and horses, all were coming together for the great blow. The whole industrial might of a great empire was concentrated on a small area of France behind twenty miles of front line.

And Haig, naturally, had by no means forgotten his trump card. All the cavalry were withdrawn to be 'fattened up' for the coming offensive. Under General Gough they charged over the downlands in intricate manœuvres.

Excitement mounted. Bets were laid as to the date of the attack (in both allied and German lines). 'We'll all be home by Christmas,' some said, as the Regulars had in 1914. Others were not so hopeful. But there was certainly a feeling that it was time to get to grips with the Hun. Only the more experienced soldiers were inclined to be a little morbid.

The general feeling was that this would not be like the dud attacks of the past. It was commonly believed that all the opposition, or at the worst most of it, would be wiped out by the British artillery before the first waves even went over the top.

General Haig visited the lines and appeared pleased with all he saw. He rode around on his splendid horse (his fluttering pennant carried by a W.O.1 of the Dragoon Guards), fantastically turned out with shining brass and tanned face, with his famous waxed and boned riding boots and his grim, determined jaw. Haig seemed like the very epitome of the courage ('pluck') that was going to be necessary when the day arrived.

Everywhere he went, Douglas Haig inspired confidence among the officers and men. One only had to look at him to see that here was a man who knew what he was doing. Soon he moved his headquarters to Beauquesne, only twelve miles back, so everyone knew it would not be long now. (Haig's customary H.Q. was at Montreuil about forty-five miles behind the front.)

Haig had in fact been picking himself a group of men who would surround him during the course of the battle. Hand-picked, he hoped they would provide a team of intellect and ability that would out-think the German staff. But Douglas Haig could seldom see if and when he was wrong, and consequently when picking men he was limited to picking those who agreed with him rather than otherwise, as those who did not would naturally be inclined to make too many mistakes.

Haig was surrounded by notorious 'Yes-men', like his chief intelligence officer, Brigadier-General Charteris, and his chief of staff, Lieutenant-General L. E. Kiggell. This was probably Haig's weakest point as a commander. He preferred to hear mumbles of assent, rather than criticisms and argument.

Rawlinson, too, was working hard at staff work at his headquarters, at Querrieux, fourteen miles behind the line. As the days went on, the pace of work became intense. He held his last conference before the battle with his corps commanders on 22 June. Nothing could be overlooked. He was still able, however, to continue his habit of going for a ride before breakfast each morning.

CHAPTER EIGHT

THE HOME FRONT

In England, meanwhile, farm workers in the fields of Kent could hear the booming of the guns on the Western Front. The war seemed to be dragging on, with no definite signs of victory. People were puzzled by the great naval battle of Jutland, at which thousands of sailors had perished in the icy seas. Had it been a victory? Or was it a defeat? Even the Admiralty did not seem to know.

Many soldiers were on leave in London, the authorities for once being generous with applications because, as everyone knew, the Push was coming soon, and it might be the last chance for a bit of Blighty for some time, or perhaps even for ever. The music-halls were doing an excellent trade, although some young officers were seen to be a little uncomfortable at the immensely patriotic, jingoistic, Hun-hating songs. Restaurants, like Romano's, had seldom known business better. Young men in uniform were to be seen at all the smart places, escorting the same adoring ladies who had 'felt they ought to go' (in the words of the 1914 song), dressed in the latest fashions.

Young soldiers on leave gazed with sad resignation, that people at home found it difficult to understand, at the shoe-shine boys in Coventry Street, at the buses going down the Strand, at the flower-sellers with their colourful baskets – all carrying on as if there was nothing unusual happening in the world.

Hospitals were being cleared and made ready throughout southern England. Convalescents were being sent away, beds prepared, wards set up in newly built huts. Vera Brittain, a V.A.D. at one of these hospitals, waiting for the wounded to start coming home, wrote: 'Hour after hour, as the convalescents departed, we added to the long rows of waiting beds, so sinister in their white, expectant emptiness.'

In St. James's Park the lake was being drained to make way way for army huts. But you could still get a room at the Metropole in Brighton, plus accommodation for chauffeur, for near ten shillings. Or you could stay at 'London's Most Recent

Hotel' for five and sixpence, which covered 'bedroom, attendance, bath and breakfast'.

The Hon. Mrs. G. Northcote was running a 'Practical Motor School for Ladies' in Kensington. The Prime Minister, Asquith, was reading. 'I alternate between frivolities like *Lolage's Lovers* (quite readable) and rather stodgy biography. There is a lot of good stuff in Q.-C.'s *Art of Writing*.' Sir William Maxwell Aitken, M.P. for Ashton-under-Lyne, had just been created a Baronet. ('He is,' explained *The Times*, 'the close friend and adviser of Mr. Bonar Law.')

Readers were encouraged to send their 'War Snapshots' to the *Daily Mail*, 'which always pays the best prices'.

Marlborough managed to stave off defeat by Winchester with only one wicket in hand. Sir Roger Casement was being tried in the High Court in a sensational case of high treason (the report took up half a page and more of *The Times*). And there was a correspondence in the same newspaper about the desecration of beauty spots by 'those who are brought from town in the motor-omnibuses'.

The theatre was having a good year, and it had to be a very bad play, or an exceptionally good one, not to get full houses. *Chu Chin Chow* was one of the most successful shows ever to have been seen on the London stage. And *Romance,* with Doris Keane and Owen Nares, was a popular 'must' for all those on leave seeking the manna of forgetfulness. Henry Ainley was at the Haymarket in a new Vachell comedy; Irene Vanbrugh was at the New in Somerset Maugham's *Caroline*. Harry Tate was doing his well-known motoring sketch at the Hippodrome; Gertie Millar was at the Palace. And at the Alhambra were André Charlot's 'Bing Boys', with George Robey singing 'If You Were the Only Girl in the World'.

But, of course, the casualty lists appeared every day, and sometimes they were long, and all over the country people searched through them anxiously – a daily torture. Some noticed that there were reports of a heavy barrage by the British artillery at 'a certain part of the Western Front'. Although no reason was given for this, they knew it might mean that the 'Big Push' was coming at last.

CHAPTER NINE

'JERRY'

MOST of the German soldiers on the Western Front in 1916 still wanted to win the war, and had every hope of doing so, whereas many French soldiers were past caring and wanted only peace. The German troops had been told that they were invincible, believed it, and believed in the inevitable march of the all-conquering German empire. The general staff, however, were realizing at the beginning of 1916 that their main enemy from now on was to be the British. When their wearing-down tactics of Verdun proved successful as the spring and summer progressed, they knew that Britain would have to take the brunt of the war.

A 'hymn of hate' was composed for the German troops, in order to put them in the right frame of mind. 'French and Russian, they matter not, we have but one and only hate, we have one foe and one alone, England.'

The German commander at the Somme, an able General named Fritz von Below, knew by February that something was going on. He suggested a large-scale attack might take place there during the year. Crown Prince Rupprecht of Bavaria started making notes in his diary about similar suspicions of his own. Soon the suspicions began to look like certainties. When the famous French Iron Corps (the XXth) was moved into the line south of the Somme, he suspected that the French also were to be in the attack.

A report was sent to the German G.H.Q. outlining the British preparations opposite Gommecourt and Fricourt (described as 'super-fortresses'), and in April a preventative attack was prepared on the Somme, in order to disturb the British plans there and to take the initiative. But it was soon decided that the men could not be spared from Verdun for this task.

On a closer study of the ground from the British point of view, von Below now had doubts as to the suspected attack, although he was unable to account for the great activity behind the British lines, which was clear to everyone with a pair of field glasses and normal eyesight.

On 15 June the Kaiser visited Rupprecht's 6th Army H.Q. at

Douai (the 6th Army held the line north of von Below). Falkenhayn was also present, and he said that he could not understand why the British should attack on the Somme. Despite all the evidence, he was baffled by the British preparations. He could not make out their intentions. Why should they wish to attack him at his strongest point? Did they imagine they would have any easier results from attrition than he was winning at Verdun? He was inclined, on this occasion, to belittle Rupprecht's warnings. If the British succeeded, he said, it was likely that further fighting would take place in Belgium, a thing that the allies would surely not want as the country would be devastated. And in any event they would not want northern France, with its important coal mines and industrial areas, laid waste.

But Rupprecht continued to report to Falkenhayn and the general staff on the obvious preparations going on behind the French and British lines. He noticed the increased railway traffic, trench construction, new artillery emplacements, and vast new camps appearing in the Albert district. Fritz von Below said that if Haig attacked he might let him through into a large salient, and then encircle or rout him by heavy attacks on his flanks.

On 1 June, Arthur Henderson, M.P., said in a speech to owners and employers of factories at Leeds:

I am asked why the Whitsuntide holidays are to be postponed until the end of July. How inquisitive we all are! It should suffice that we ask for a postponement of the Holidays until the end of July. This fact should speak volumes!

At Sheffield on the same day, Dr. Addison, Parliamentary Secretary to Lloyd George's Ministry of Munitions, made a similar speech. He did not, he said, make his appeal for a postponement of the holiday lightly, or without good cause, and he had good reason for asking it in the way he did. Lloyd George, he said, asked for their trust in the matter.

The two speeches were widely reported in all the London newspapers of 2 June, which were read with interest by the German intelligence staff. They arrived in Berlin in forty-eight hours, via Holland.

Rupprecht told the Kaiser that an agent in the Hague reported that the British military attaché there had said that the coming British offensive on the Somme would take place very soon. On 24 June, a prisoner of the British 42nd Division was captured at Gommecourt. He stated that a five days' bombardment would begin on the 26th, and an attack on a thirty-mile front would begin on 1 July. The Crown Prince dutifully recorded this in his diary.

By now, it was accepted by all the German commanders that a great British assault of the German line was to take place at the Somme. Everyone knew it, from Falkenhayn to the most insignificant private in the trenches. Rupprecht noted: 'French papers, especially *La Victoire,* write a good deal about the impending British offensive, in which at last the great British Army, the work of Kitchener, will make a decisive attack and show what it can do.'

Von Below asked for reserves to beat off the attack. Despite the pressure on German manpower at Verdun, 'his demands were met as fully as possible', Falkenhayn later recorded.

On 26 June, the German military attaché at Madrid, and a secret agent, reported independently that the attack would begin on 1 July. A German pilot flew over the British line and carefully studied the practice of the attack that was to take place on Gommecourt a few days later.

On 27 June, Rupprecht noted: 'North of the Somme, 14 captive balloons have been counted, corresponding to the 14 British divisions in line there.' Wavell's desperate efforts were to have an effect that he had not intended.

The German positions were well-nigh perfect. On a long crest, they were able to look down on the allied trenches in the dip below. The previous winter, when they had pumped water from their flooded dugouts, it had run down into the allied positions. This ridge was not a straight one but consisted of several spurs. The tops of these spurs had been turned into seige fortresses, stronger than any others on the whole Western Front. There were woods and villages on the spurs and they, also, had been heavily fortified. As there had been no serious fighting here since 1914, the Germans had occupied themselves by building what must have seemed to them an almost impregnable fort.

The fortifications along the ridge and spurs had been constructed with great subtlety, so that there were few places where an attack would not come under crossfire. Subterranean passages had been constructed, leading to machine-gun emplacements in the side of spurs. Dug-outs of thirty and even forty feet had been built. All this had been simplified by the chalk soil of the Somme valley.

In the dug-outs and deep trenches, there were electric light and washing apparatus, surgeries and hospital wards in bomb-proof cellars, pulleys, steel rails with trucks for ammunition, stairs with wired treads, air and escape shafts. The living-rooms, which had panelled walls, were decorated with cretonnes of the smartest Berlin patterns, and had neat bunks and furniture.

Well behind the lines were many old caves and underground passages which had been made years before to gain chalk for building purposes. Now they provided excellent shelter for German reserves.

The system consisted of two lines, each with several rows of trenches, and a third one in preparation. Before each was run an extremely formidable barrier of wire. This wire was in belts of twenty to thirty yards' thickness and had barbs as thick as a man's thumb. Staked down with iron posts, it already had its souvenirs, the stragglers of odd raiding parties, which hung on it like dilapidated scarecrows.

Although the first German line could be seen or estimated from the forward British trenches, it was impossible to see the second line, or its wire. It was thus extremely difficult to tell how effective any barrage was in destroying that wire. These two trench systems were about two to three miles apart.

The Germans, on the other hand, could see practically everything going on in the British lines, and behind them. They were able to see all the four roads leading from Albert to the front, and could shell them accurately.

The British attempts at camouflage were ludicrously inadequate. The camouflage unit of the army, consisting of a few carpenters, painters, and artists, was not officially sanctioned until 22 March. They attempted to screen roads here and there by means of broad strips of canvas hung up on wires. Snipers' suits were made, and green and brown machine-gun covers. Artificial trees were prepared for observation posts or periscopes; but as the battlefield was soon to be made treeless, their possibilities were limited.

The projecting fortresses on the German line started, in the north, at Gommecourt, a fortified wood and village. Many considered this the strongest position in France. On 1 July Allenby's Third Army was to stage a diversionary attack on it. About four miles to the south, the second projection occurred

at the village of Beaumont Hamel. Below this the Germans
had built another strong fort. The Schwaben redoubt at the
head of the next spur, looked straight down on the British
trenches. Next to it was a dip known as Crucifix Valley. The
village of Thiepval was at the top of a slope on the south side
of the Ancre, a tributary of the Somme, looking down on the
river and the British trenches. Beyond it was the Leipzig
Salient, a narrow spur, across the end of which ran an extremely strong trench, known as the Hohenzollern. From it the
German troops could see to the other side of Albert. Ovillers,
La Boisselle, and Fricourt were other fortified villages jutting
out of the German line.

After Fricourt, the German line curved down to the Somme.
Behind this ridge of spurs on which was the German first line,
there was another. On this was the second line. The slopes of
this second ridge were dotted with thick woods; Mametz, Delville, Trones, Bernafay, and High Wood.

Throughout most of the battle the British troops were fated
to have the enemy troops above them; always they had to
trudge upwards. These kind of conditions are the most depressing under which infantry can fight.

On the French sector the ground was more level, there being
very little difference in height between the two sides. For over
six miles south of the Somme, the German line ran almost in
a straight line, with no appreciable spurs.

The natural strength of the German position facing the
British sector was greatly strengthened by the depths of their
dug-outs. This was, indeed, the crucial fact of the whole battle.
Deep down in their shelters the Germans could play cards
while the Royal Artillery sent over thousands of shells, the
explosions of which did not even spill the beer from German
mugs. The depth of these shelters was a surprise to all the
British troops, when they were eventually taken, from Haig
to private soldiers.

During May and June the Germans practised bringing up
their machine-guns and themselves from the dug-outs in a
few minutes. Apart from a few sentries, their line could be
deserted, and then three minutes later fully manned. As soon
as their protective wire was seriously cut, the Germans detailed
another machine-gun crew to train their weapon on the gap.

By the middle of June, all England was discussing the 'Big
Push'. Everyone knew it was coming; that was common know-

ledge. The only thing that people were not quite sure of was the exact day of attack.

The German Command, of course, was in a better position. Although they already knew the battle was about to begin, they must have received with some wry comments the actual last message of the British Commander, Rawlinson, to his troops. This was picked up on 1 July, at two forty-five a.m. Berlin time, by a listening-post near La Boisselle, and promptly reported to an underground regimental H.Q.

The message wished all ranks of the Fourth Army 'Good luck'.

CHAPTER TEN

MAKING IT EASY

If the artillery did its work well, said General Rawlinson, the rest would be easy.

A careful programme of artillery bombardment had been worked out. Like the plan for the infantry, it was precise, exact and left no room for last-minute changes to account for unforeseen circumstances. The programme was to be in a number of stages. It was to last for five days, immediately preceeding zero day; the first two of which were to be mainly concerned with wire-cutting, the following three with the destruction of defences and continued wire-cutting.

Every day there was to be a concentrated bombardment of eighty minutes during which the enemy would be presumed to have taken cover. But on zero day the bombardment was to be a quarter of an hour shorter – the assault to take place immediately after – the assumption being that this would find the enemy unprepared.

There was also to be a certain amount of bombing by the R.F.C. It was intended to flatten such villages as still stood behind the German line. It is interesting that in a military handbook still read in 1916, *Land Warfare: An exposition of the Laws and Usages of War on Land for the Guidance of Officers of his Majesty's Army*, it is stated that 'it is not sufficient reason for bombardment that a town contains supplies of value to the enemy, or railway establishments, telegraphs, or bridges. These must, if it is necessary to do so, be destroyed by other means.' But, alas, the laws and usages of war were all going by the board every day on the Western Front.

The great bombardment duly began at six a.m. on 24 June. The vibrations were felt in Camberwell. Apart from the eighty-minute concentrated bombardment, it was also arranged that the German line would continuously be under some sort of artillery fire night and day. The German retaliation was comparatively feeble; when they replied, they were often given two shells back for every one of theirs. At ten o'clock on the night of the 24th an order was given for a discharge of gas. There was, fortunately for the Germans, almost no wind, and

local commanders decided not to send it over, except in the
4th Division. On release at that part of the front, the gas did
in fact drift very slowly across to the German trenches. The
gas was kept up for an hour. The Germans retaliated with
exceptionally heavy artillery fire. (A French gunner played
Beethoven on the violin through it all.)

The barrage continued on the 25th, 26th, and 27th. But
things were not going quite as expected. There had been occur-
rences for which no arrangements had been made in the strict
plan. The weather was not good; there were showers and
mists, which made observation of fire difficult. The crews
of many of the heavy batteries had only recently arrived at the
front and their observation officers had not had sufficient time
to study the land. At three-thirty p.m. on the 26th the bombardment had to be stopped for a short time to enable the
R.F.C. to fly over and take photographs; but the art of reading air photographs was still in its infancy.

It soon appeared that there were not enough heavy guns.
The lighter guns were having little effect, except, it was hoped,
in wire-cutting. Lloyd George had actually exceeded the supply
asked for by the War Office in the heavy calibres, and had met
with disapproval from Kitchener for doing so. But there still
were not enough. There were only 104 six-inch howitzers, for
instance. In the Battle of Messines, the following year, on a
front only about two-thirds as long, there were 348. There
was, however, one enormous gun, mounted on the railway
behind Albert, which did some damage from thirteen miles
range.

Much of the ammunition was American, and of a low standard. The remainder had been manufactured hurriedly at home,
under Lloyd George's constant goadings. Premature bursts
destroyed guns and crews. There were frequent appalling
scenes on the artillery lines with bits of mutilated bodies flying
about over the gunners. An immense strain was put on all the
crews; men had to be rested after two-hour periods. The 4.5
howitzer crews called themselves 'The Suicide Club', so frequent were the explosions of defective ammunition.

It became clear that the wire was not being cut as much as it
had been hoped. But local commanders had no power to
switch their fire to further wire-cutting, even when it was
plainly a matter of life and death. The French officers had
greater freedom, and, as was their custom, some elasticity had
been left in their barrage programme.

As the bombardment continued it was obvious to all, Germans and British, that at last the Push was about to begin. British troops stood on the hills behind their lines and cheered as the explosions sounded. It looked as if their job, for once, was really being made easy.

At night-time, last-minute raiding parties were sent out to get information about the effects of the barrage, as the flashes of the guns lit up the night sky. These were exceedingly dangerous expeditions, leading to considerable loss of life. Their reports were conflicting. Two patrols of the 29th Division reported the enemy line 'very much damaged', and another two 'not much damaged'. But there was one consistency in nearly all reports; the wire was still there, hardly damaged at all.

The weather continued bad, and at eleven a.m. on the 28th it was decided to delay the attack until 1 July. This meant an extra two days' bombardment, which had not been allowed for in the original calculations. Altogether 1,508,652 shells were fired in the barrage. The heavy guns, the only ones that really mattered, had to economize. The wire in front of Thiepval and Gommecourt still appeared to observers in the front trenches to be entirely intact. Practically every division, in fact, reported that wire-cutting in its sector had not been satisfactory. But by now the main concentration of fire was on the communication systems and the German front trenches.

The few Germans who were sent up on sentry duty from the dug-outs were going to something close to suicide. One prisoner told John Masefield (an official observer):

Those who went outside were killed or wounded. Some of them had their heads blown off, some of them had had both their legs torn off, and some of them their arms. But we went on taking turns in the hole, although those who went outside knew that it was their turn to die, most likely.

All German accounts speak of the shock of this bombardment, despite their deep shelters. They had not undergone such a heavy barrage so far in the war, and despite the safety in which the majority of them were, the noise was deafening, and the fumes stifling. Some of them got shell shock; fits of trembling and weeping. Some giggled and muttered to themselves, others became dull at every sharp command. For most it was a horrifying experience, and they longed for the start of the battle.

CHAPTER ELEVEN

GETTING ON PARADE

'COMPANY to parade in battle order!' The command rang out down twenty miles of line; in hamlets, in support trenches, in camps of hut and tent, in woods and meadows. The time had come.

During the bombardment the line had been held by machine-gun, mortar, and reserve companies. On the morning of 30 June, the infantry companies were relieved and last preparations were made. Messages of encouragement were read to the men. In some brigades, ceremonial parades were held, with bands playing, flags flying, and ending in a march past. Provost police took up posts to deal with stragglers in the great movement of bringing the army up to the front trenches that was now to take place.

These were the lucky ones. Because of the two days' postponement some battalions, already in the trenches by 29 June, had to remain there for two days and nights, before they went over the top – some of the men having only the haziest idea of what was happening. As it had rained heavily on the 28th and 29th, many of the trenches were flooded. Miserable, soaked, hungry, they waited. But according to the *Official History*, 'although many men felt ill, very few reported themselves sick, for fear that they might miss the great day'.

Patrols and raiding parties were sent out as usual on the nights of the 29th and 30th in an attempt to make the Germans think nothing untoward was taking place; what they were expected to make of the quite unprecedented barrage, Haig alone knew. Some of these parties, however, did perform a useful service in cutting their own wire. Serving in the first battalion of the Royal Welch Fusiliers, Siegfried Sassoon wrote:

> When we did get started I soon discovered that cutting tangles of barbed wire in the dark in a desperate hurry is a job that needs ingenuity, even when your wire-cutters have rubber-covered handles and are fresh from the Army and Navy Stores. More than once we were driven in by shells which landed in front of our trench (some of them were our

71

own dropping short); two men were wounded and some of the others were reluctant to resume work. In the first greying of dawn only three of us were still at it ... but as the light increased I began to realize the unimpressive effect of the snippings and snatchings which had made such a mess of our leather gloves. We had been working three and a half hours, but the hedge hadn't suffered much damage it seemed.

Later, on his own initiative, Sasson went out to complete the job in broad daylight. 'It was', he later recorded in *Memoirs of an Infantry Officer,* 'rather like going out to weed a neglected garden after being warned that there might be a tiger among the gooseberry bushes.' Sassoon was, by all accounts, an astonishly brave young officer. He was awarded the M.C. the day before the battle began.

Every infantryman assembled his 'fighting order' and strapped himself up in it. This included: steel helmet, entrenchment tool, rolled groundsheet, water bottle, haversack (with mess tin, towel, shaving kit, extra socks, message books, cheese, and preserved rations), two gas helmets, tear goggles, wire-cutters, field dressing and iodine, two bandoliers of small arms ammunition, and a rifle.

The total equipment per man was meant to be about sixty-six pounds; in fact it was a good deal more, because of various odd articles which were distributed amoung them, such as picks, shovels (fifty to the leading companies), sand-bags, Mills grenades, carrier-pigeon boxes, telephones, and ladders. Officers and N.C.O.s also carried four flares each.

Says the *Official History:*

The total weight ... made it difficult to get out of a trench impossible to move much quicker than a slow walk, or to rise and lie down quickly. This overloading of the men is by many infantry officers regarded as one of the principal reasons for the heavy losses and failure of their battalions; for their men could not get through the machine-gun zone with sufficient speed.

Various detailed instructions had been issued, from Rawlinson's Operation Order down to battalion details.

The Operation Order started: 'The Fourth Army will take part in a general offensive with a view to breaking up the enemy's defensive system, and of exploiting to the full all opportunities opened up for defeating his forces within easy reach.' It continued in a similar elusive fashion.

Other instructions stated that prisoners were to be escorted on a scale of ten per cent of their numbers; that all ranks were forbidden to divert their attention from the enemy in order to attend wounded officers or men; that flares were to be fired in answer to long klaxon blasts from R.F.C. planes (which meant 'who and where are you?'); that in the front trenches there should be a ladder to every two men, which were to be placed in position just before zero – the man on the right to go first; that boards in German trenches would be torn up and placed as bridges over the parapets for following waves; that 'Battle Police' would see to it that no one would 'lose their way'; that 'most extreme disciplinary action will be taken in the case of any officer, N.C.O. or private found in possession of any article taken from the dead.'

It was nothing unusual on the Western Front that these orders were mostly shrugged at, scoffed, and frequently ignored. If they were obeyed to the letter, staff orders could often mean certain death. This strengthened the feeling of men and officers in the trenches that they were living in a world of their own, to which even the laws of nature no longer applied, and into which no 'red tabs' could ever, or would ever, enter.

Some of the orders were optimistic. It was advised that under no conditions would the display of white flags by the enemy call for any cease fire. The matter would be reported to Divisional H.Q., and firing would continue.

During the night of 30 June, under bright stars, the Fourth Army took up its battle positions. It was a moonless summer night, and the routes were marked out with tapes and posts, or green and red lanterns. Officers had previously reconnoitred the way, but the back area of the Somme line was a complicated maze of trenches, aid posts, dumps, batteries, local H.Q.s, and shell craters. The nightly bombardment drowned any noise. Slowly they filed down into the trenches and sheltered assembly points, packing them with overladen bodies. Between three and five-fifteen a.m. most of them found their positions, after a good deal of cursing and confusion.

Sassoon recalls:

There was a congestion of troops in the support trench outside our dug-out. They had lost their way, and I remembered how the exhausted men propped themselves against the sides of the trench while their exasperated Adjutant and a confused civilian Colonel grumbled about the ambiguity of their operation orders. They were to attack on our left, and they vanished in that direction, leaving me with my Military Cross and a foreboding that disaster awaited them. Since they came within the limited zone of my observations I can record the fact that they left their trench early next morning at a wrong zero hour and got badly cut up by the artillery support which ought to have made things easy for them.

As the rear troops moved up through the choked, battered streets of Albert, the Golden Virgin gleamed over them in every gun flash. On the whole, the German batteries were fairly quiet, although the northern part of the line, opposite the Gommecourt salient, suffered quite heavily on their assembly trenches, over which a German pilot had flown not long before. This comparative lack of heavy German fire made commanders and men hope that there was to be some surprise, and that the British bombardment had done its work in flattening and demoralizing the enemy.

As they reached the trenches, the troops were fed, as their next mealtime was uncertain, and soup-containers were brought up carried on a pole slung between two men. Bully beef, biscuits, bread and jam, tea, and cheese were consumed by those who had the stomach for them.

Although there were the normal feelings of fear and expectancy that existed before any large offensive, the general feeling in the trenches during the early hours of 1 July 1916 was one of confidence in the barrage that had made so much noise. It cancelled out the few misgivings about the late hour of attack which was to take place at seven-thirty in full daylight. Rawlinson and Haig had wished for an attack in the dawn, and had pressed the idea on the French, but they had insisted on a later hour, in order that their observers could clearly see the results of the final bombardment.

Says the *Official History*:

It may be accepted that the troops, as a whole, believed that the enemy's defences had been destroyed; his wire shot away, and all his efforts to rejoin it stopped by bursts of shrapnel and machine-gun fire; his trenches levelled or reduced to a chasm of shell holes; his dug-outs knocked in;

his machine-gun emplacements and observation posts smashed up.

Not all the officers, however, felt happy about their orders. Commanding officers in the Ulster Division had received instructions not to accompany their men in the attack, but to take to their dug-outs so as to be 'safe'. F. P. Crozier was commanding officer of a battalion of the Royal Irish Rifles. He wrote: 'The whole idea was repulsive. It cut right across the foundations of mutual trust, emphasized in training, between private soldier and officer.' Together with the C.O. of his neighbouring battalion, he protested, to no avail. 'The indecent order had come from high up in the hierarchy – and well back.' The two officers agreed to disobey it. 'Our plan was to meet in No Man's Land, if alive. There we would supervise the deployment and make any necessary alterations in the plan over which we had little control.'

There was a close bond between officers and men in most battalions on the Western Front, especially those of the New Army. They shared a secret of horror that no civilian would ever fully understand. The closeness and understanding was helped by the censorship, in which officers read the heart-pourings of their men.

As the sun rose behind the gentle slopes of the Somme valley, a slight, fine-weather, misty haze accompanied it. It looked as if it was going to be a perfect, hot summer's day.

All neatly docketed and tagged, the men waited; their helmets marked with regimental and divisional signs; on their shoulder-straps the coloured ribbons of their companies; and a regimental device on a small piece of cloth sewn beneath the back of their collars.

To some it seemed absurd to eat, when they might be dead in an hour or two. Self-preservation directed another oiling of the bolt. As the minutes went on, watches were consulted more often, talking became less, but cigarette smoking increased. In the breaks of barrage, the distant sounds of trains could be heard.

John Masefield mixed with the survivors of 1 July shortly afterwards and faithfully recorded their thoughts and emotions as they waited to go over the top. He tells how two of them had a bet of cigarettes about the position of a sniper who had been causing heavy casualties in their sector. 'When I go over, I thought, we'll see who'll get them fags.'

Said another: 'Half an hour before we went over they got on to our jumping-off trenches and fairly plugged us with a lot of heavy stuff as well; so I said: you —s, you wait till I get in among you, I'll get some of my own back.'

An officer told Masefield: 'Some of my men were cursing and mad; I don't think they knew what they were doing, but about every other man was praying.'

A soldier remembered: 'I made up in my mind I was going to be killed.' During the last half hour he kept saying, every few minutes, 'In twenty minutes I'll be dead,' and so on. He found himself envying those who would go to bed that night, those he had seen behind the line. He felt 'ache, and anger and a longing to be alive'. He thought he heard a lark among the noise. A rat ran down the trench among the men and they hit out at it, but it got away.

Another survivor told Masefield:

My sergeant really seemed to enjoy it. He was about forty-five and smoking a pipe, and talking about South Africa. I thought this is what life is, you get together with a lot of other fellows in a pub or somewhere, and swap a story or two about the blackguards you have known, and then you go out and get knocked on the head by a set of corner boys.

Another said:

I tried to tell myself that I was doing it for this or that reason, to make it sound better, but I didn't believe those grand things. When you are waiting to be killed, those damned newspapers seem damned thin, and so do those damned poems about the Huns. The Fritzes are a dirty lot, but they are damned brave, you may say what you like. And being killed by a lot of damned Fritzes is damned bad egg, and no amount of talk will alter it.

As they waited, and thought and prayed, and looked up at the parapet, and the brightening sky, and fingered their equipment, they hummed songs to give themselves courage. 'Whiter Than the Whitewash on the Wall,' 'If the Sergeant Drinks Your Rum, Never Mind,' 'I've Lost My Rifle and Bayonet.' Songs of others' misfortunes were always encouraging.

Faintly, in the morning air, between shell blasts, a gramophone could be heard playing across in a German dug-out.

Considering how bashed about their line was thought to be, it was a macabre noise.

Twelve miles away, at Beauquesne, Sir Douglas Haig was fast asleep. But soon he would be up and about, eating an early breakfast, and waiting anxiously for the first reports. Before going to bed, he had written up his diary:

> The weather report is favourable for tomorrow. With God's help, I feel hopeful. The men are in splendid spirits. Several have said that they have never before been so instructed and informed of the nature of the operation before them. The wire has never been so well cut, nor the Artillery preparations so thorough.

Haig had visited the corps commanders and found that 'one and all are full of confidence'. This was strange, bearing in mind what some of them had to say afterwards. As for Rawlinson, he thought the whole thing 'a gamble'. And Charteris, the intelligence officer, who had been steadily supplying Haig with the encouraging reports that he wished to hear, thought that the army was about to embark on a long and weary battle. Haig himself fully expected to get, at least, the second German line on the first day, and possible a notable break-through.

So much for the expectations. Now the inevitable moment was drawing near. Nothing on earth could have stopped it.

Across in the German trenches, last-minute orders were being made about the coming attack. Rawlinson's 'Good luck' message was received. A hurried evacuation of a stronghold known as the 'Y Sap' was carried out. Beneath it, they knew, was a mine, likely to be set off just before zero.

From 6.25 a.m. onwards there was an incessant earthquake of artillery fire. Shells screamed and whistled over the waiting troops. They burst, with great explosions, all along the German line, in No Man's Land, and even on the British trenches. It was almost impossible to talk, so great was the din. Some men half-heartedly cheered, believing this final blow must have finished what chance there was left of any opposition. Eight minutes before zero the mortars joined in, firing thirty rounds a minute each.

The order was given: 'Fix bayonets.'

The clinking of steel sounded down miles of narrow, twisting trench.

The mines went off with dull thuds, or loud explosions, all adding to the deafening row. Men were breathing quickly, and swallowing often. Some shook hands. Some were sick. Seven-thirty showed on the dials of thousands of watches. Flasks appeared as if from nowhere. Suddenly the barrage lifted; there was a strange, uncanny silence. With cocked rifles slung over their right shoulders, an army of over a hundred thousand city clerks, farm hands, solicitors, miners, and barrow-boys went over the top.

CHAPTER TWELVE

THE PUSH

ALONG most of the eighteen-mile front, men were met with heavy machine-gun fire a few seconds after they had clambered up the ladders and swarmed over the parapets, through their own wire and into No Man's Land. It did not take long for the German gunners to scramble up from their dug-outs as soon as the barrage lifted to their rear at seven-thirty. On some parts of the front the attackers were met by heavy artillery barrage as well as machine-gun fire.

As they went over the top into the hailstorm of bullets, men mumbled prayers, stepped over corpses, pushed aside dead bodies of their comrades that fell back down the ladders, screamed out for 'stretcher bearers', and many knew already that it was going to be worse than any had expected. Bits of limbs flew about in the air. A leg, with puttee streaming behind it, landed in the wire. Some men could go no farther and sat down and wept.

But all down the front the attack pushed on towards the German wire and the first enemy trench. As the soldiers fell, thousands more were incessantly pouring over to take their places. Steadily the decimated, always thinning line pressed on.

In some places junior officers waved on their men with whistles jammed in their teeth piercing above the scream of battle. In other places, it had been ordered that 'strict silence' would be maintained during the advance and no whistles were to be blown.

Once they had left the trenches and got through the British wire in single file, the remaining troops lined up shoulder to shoulder and walked on into the fire, carrying their useless rifles. Owing to the weight of equipment, at no point in the whole advance was any attempt made to run. Wincing and blinking, shouting and cursing, they stumbled on under the blazing sun.

F. P. Crozier led his battalion in the second wave.

I get up from the ground and whistle. The others rise. We move off with steady pace. I see rows upon rows of British soldiers lying dead, dying or wounded in No Man's Land. Here and there I see an officer urging on his followers. Occasionally I can see the hands thrown up and then a body flops on the ground. The bursting shells and smoke make visibility poor. We proceed. Again I look southward from a different angle and perceive heaped up masses of British corpses suspended on the German wire, while live men rush forward in orderly procession to swell the weight of numbers in the spider's web. We march on – I lose sight of the 10th Rifles and the human corn-stalks falling before the reaper ... 'This way to eternity' shouts a wag behind ... now a shell – plomp – a splinter flies past my shoulder, and embeds itself in the leg of a leading man behind. He falls and crawls out of the way, nothing must stop the forward march of the column. 'Lucky b———' says one of his pals. This spirited dash across No Man's Land has cost us some 50 dead and 70 disabled.

From behind the British lines, on the rear slopes, observers had an extraordinary view of the whole assault. Men, like dots, could be seen stopping everywhere, and the great brown wave disintegrating after a few hundred yards, into isolated groups and individual dots. One of the observers was Siegfried Sassoon, resting in reserve after his wire-cutting efforts. He wrote in his diary as he watched:

7.45. Our men in small parties go steadily on to the German front line. Brilliant sunshine and a haze of smoke drifting along the landscape. Some Yorkshires a little way below on the left watching the show and cheering as if it were a football match. The noise almost as bad as ever. The sunlight flashes on bayonets as the tiny figures move quietly forward and disappear beyond mounds of trench debris.

9.45. Fricourt half-hidden by clouds of drifting smoke, blue, pinkish and grey. Shrapnel bursting in small bluish-white puffs with tiny flashes. The birds seem bewildered; a lark begins to go up and then flies feebly along, thinking better of it.

Later in the morning, Sassoon wrote:

I can see the Manchesters down in New Trench, getting ready to go over. Figures filing down the trench. Two of them have gone out to look at our wire gaps! Have just eaten my last orange ... I am staring at a sunlit picture of

Hell, and still the breeze shakes the yellow weeds, and the poppies glow under Crawley Ridge where some shell fell a few minutes ago. A bayonet glitters. Heavy shelling towards Mametz. Weather cloudless and hot.

Manchesters left New Trench ... Many walked casually across with sloped arms. There were about forty casualties on the left. Through my glasses I could see one man moving his left arm up and down as he lay on his side; his face was a crimson patch. Others lay still in the sunlight while the swarm of figures disappeared over the hill. At 2.50 no one to be seen in No Man's Land except the casualties.

In fact, long before two fifty, the battle at which Sassoon had been able to look with such detachment was already lost for the British. Survivors were back in the trenches from which they had started; or in the German first trench, but cut off from supplies, reinforcements or instructions; or lying still in No Man's Land. Almost half those who went over the top on 1 July were killed or wounded.

Many lay wounded in No Man's Land, shrieking for water, with no attention likely to come; others lay there pretending to be dead. A good deal of this ground was still covered by the machine-gunners on the spurs in the German line, even though at a few places British troops had succeeded in reaching the German trenches.

As stretcher bearers came out to collect the wounded, they came under fire, and they had no option but to wait till nightfall. Planes hovered above, as pilots peered at the scene below, trying to make out what progress, if any, had been made. Only one hour after the attack nearly everywhere there was complete confusion. In the German trenches a few parties of British fought desperately for hours trying to hold on to their bloodily won gains. Most of their fighting was done with bombs. They were bound to run out. One man bringing up more bombs and braving the hazards of No Man's Land with a jacket full of bombs, was blown to pieces. Orders were not being received. Parties of mixed soldiers from various battalions fought on, or retreated, according to their own decisions; groups in No Man's Land planned for escape to the British trenches at nightfall.

Some men were lost. Trenches all looked much alike. Landmarks of yesterday had disappeared. Whole battalions, or the remnants of them, wandered around in haphazard directions; in one case as much as half a mile behind the German line. But because of the German artillery and the many remaining machine-gunners, it was now as unsafe to retreat as it was to advance. The horrors of No Man's Land were increased by large quantities of unexploded shells lying around and by various traps near the German wire (including at least one bear trap). Primitive flame-throwers were used; a small group of British scaling a German stronghold were burnt to death.

Men caught in the wire, which was found nearly everywhere to be intact, or more so than not, ripped off their clothes and lay, half-naked, waiting for nightfall. It was impossible to discover whether one naked man was German or British when he was taken back to the British line. He was insane.

Some wounded tried to crawl back, through the tall grass speckled with poppies and wild flowers. But as the desolation increased the more difficult it became. A few hours before, yellow ragwort and blue cornflowers had lain in No Man's Land, but now, as the shelling increased, such things were quickly disappearing. Survivors huddled in craters. The majority of wounded lay out all day; sun-baked, parched, uncared for, often delirious and in agony. For the unwounded there was nothing to do but pray and dream of another, distant world called 'Blighty'.

A.D. Gristwood recalled, in the third person, his thoughts as he lay in No Man's Land.

He remembered that this was Sunday ... and thought of hymn singing in church, where the sun filled the air with the smell of warm varnish. No doubt his father was dozing after his dinner in his easy chair with mouth agape and waistcoat unbuttoned. Outside the bees were busy with the flowers, and the cat was sleeping in the sunshine. What a fool he was to be there – what fools they all were.

John Masefield, soon afterwards, collected the thoughts of those who had lain out under fire on 1 July.

Said one: 'I thought my last hour had come. They'd got a machine-gun every five yards, it sounded like. "By God," I said, "give me London every time." '

It was the opinion of another that, 'There'll be some queer revelations about this war after it's all over. I often thought of that when we were in it; not about the soldiers so much, but about the financiers.'

One told how, when they had got back to their own trenches, a 'Boche' had come over with a red-cross flag. They thought he was going to collect their wounded; but instead he calmly collected their dead comrades' Lewis guns.

Sir Douglas Haig wrote in his diary: 'Reports up to 8.0 a.m. seemed most satisfactory. Our troops had everywhere crossed the enemy's front trenches.' After having his lunch at the usual time, he motored over to Querrieux to see Sir Henry Rawlinson. As yet, no one had a clear idea of what had happened.

In London, not so far away (or so it seemed to those in London), there was great excitement at the news that the offensive that everyone had been expecting for weeks had been launched at last. Newspaper boys selling afternoon editions ran up and down the pavements excitedly shouting. Huge posters announced:

GREAT BRITISH OFFENSIVE BEGINS

At about half-past seven this morning a vigorous offensive was launched by the British Army. The front extends over about 20 miles north of the Somme. It is yet too early to give anything but the barest particulars.

Nearly every British family had a member or a close friend on the Somme that day. There was a feeling of apprehension throughout the country – long days of searching through casualty lists lay ahead. But, nevertheless, that evening London was wild with excitement. The music-halls were even gayer and noisier than usual. The bars were full.

'Our boys' were fighting at the Somme. The new armies were in action. Perhaps now, at long last, they were going to get hold of the Kaiser by the scruff of the neck, and give him a thorough shaking.

To take a closer look at what happened to the Fourth Army on 1 July, it will be convenient to look at each section of the front under the six army corps involved (one of them being, in fact, under Allenby's Third Army).

On the northern end of the attack was Allenby's VII Corps. Their part of the offensive was to be a purely diversionary one. It was meant to mislead the enemy; to make him think that this was to be the centre of the coming attack, and not farther south, and to keep his forces engaged, thus not allowing him

THE SOMME
1916

N

JULY 1

ALLENBY 3RD

VII • Gommecourt

• Bapaume

• Serre

VIII

GOUGH 5TH (FROM JULY 2)

Beaumont Hamel
• Beaucourt   × Butte de Warlencourt
                le Sars •
St. Pierre Divion   NOV 19
• Thiepval   Courcelette

                • Flers
        Martinpuich
X   • Pozières   High Wood

RAWLINSON 4TH   • Ovillers   Bazentin   Delville Wood
                        Longueval • Ginchy
        • la Boiselle
                    • Guillemont
Albert • III
Amiens—13 M.   • Montauban
        Fricourt •   • Mametz
XV   JULY 2
• Meaulte   XIII   • Maricourt

R. Ancre

FAYOLLE

XX

1 Col.

R. Somme

                        • Peronne

XXXV

R. Somme

0 1 2 3 4 5 6 7 8 9 10 MILES

to reinforce the line to the south. Accordingly, the Corps was instructed to make all its preparations as obvious as possible. These instructions were faithfully carried out, no attempt being made at concealment or surprise. Apparently Haig had no intention of making any tactical gain on this part of the front.

Unfortunately, this attack had to take place against the Gommecourt Salient, which stuck out into the British line like a great nose. It was probably the strongest position on the whole of the front; an incredibly strong, modern fortress. If an attack is to be carried out for the sole purpose of keeping enemy troops engaged and keeping them from reinforcing the line elsewhere, then it is a better policy to select a weak position rather than one already immensely strong. Allenby, indeed, suggested to Haig that a better place for this purpose would be at Arras, but his suggestion was turned down. He was, alas, the last man Haig was likely to listen to.

In its less important role the VII Corps received none of the facilities of the Fourth Army. Its lot was a wretched one. Lack of labour units made necessary the employment of nearly all the attacking troops in exhausting digging and other labour work, right up almost to the moment of attack. In one of the two attacking divisions, probably not a single man had a full night's sleep for a week before the battle.

The German troops, on the other hand, were living in comparative luxury in deep concrete dug-outs (forty feet deep), supplied with kitchens, electricity, and bunks. Their force on the salient, which Haig found so important to have engaged on 1 July, consisted of no more than nine battalions, with one in reserve.

Four days before the attack, Haig was delighted to hear from the corps commander, 'They know we are coming all right.' German records speak of the minute preparations for the coming attack. Three and a half hours before it was launched they poured down a heavy barrage on the VII Corps' forward trenches.

Of the two divisions, the 56th Division (London), did probably the better. Despite heavy losses in getting across, remnants of several battalions reached the German lines, and held them for some hours, completely cut off from their support troops and their own lines. As long as hand-grenades lasted they were able to stay there, but by midday they were sending out repeated messages: 'SOS Bombs'. From one o'clock onwards, men started coming back, straggling in small parties, or crawling across No Man's Land on their own. By the evening there were only five British officers and seventy men remaining in the German line. At nine-thirty their ammunition ran out and they, too, returned.

The other division, the 46th, completely failed in its attack; in it two battalions of the Sherwood Foresters suffered eighty per cent killed.

The attack on the Gommecourt Salient had been a hopeless one from the start. The surprising thing was that the German trenches were ever entered at all, and held for as long as they were without support. By evening on 1 July, the VII Corps was back where it had started at seven-thirty. It had lost seven thousand men, for no reason whatever – as once the intention was known to have been observed by the Germans it would have been enough that they would have been forced to hold their troops there in case the attack developed.

Below the VII Corps of Allenby's Army was the northern-most corps of Rawlinson's Army, the VIII. This corps also opposed a large salient, not quite as sharp as the Gommecourt one; a large, rounded bulge. It, too, was immensely strong. Near the top of the salient was the village of Beaumont Hamel, and about half a mile behind the line was the village of Serre, around which ran the second German line.

At the top of the salient was the Hawthorn Redoubt, a strong-point commanding a deadly view. A tunnel had been run from behind the British lines to beneath this strong-point and forty thousand pounds of ammonal lay waiting at its end for 1 July. This mine had an important bearing on the day's battle. The commander of VIII Corps wished to fire the mine four hours before zero so that the resulting crater could be occupied before zero, making a stepping-off place before the attack. The Inspector of Mines was against this, and on his advice Haig forbade the idea. It was thought that at zero the Germans were more likely to be in possession of the crater, a movement at which their adroitness was well known, rather than the British. The Inspector of Mines insisted that zero was the best time. It had previously been ordered to all corps that mines were to be exploded not more than eight minutes before zero. In this case ten minutes before zero was agreed on, as a sort of compromise.

It was still possible to occupy the crater before zero, if the mine was to be exploded at seven-twenty. But in this case it was clear that all artillery fire in the area would also have to cease at seven-twenty rather than seven-thirty, or those occupying the crater would come under the fire of their own guns.

The mine was fired at seven-twenty, and the Germans reached the crater at the same time as the British. The barrage also lifted at seven-twenty. The enemy had ten minutes in which to come up from shelter, train their machine-guns on the gaps in the wire, and generally prepare themselves before the assault. Hardly a British shell was fired at the German parapets for several hours. The troops were able to stand up, out in front of the trenches, firing as they pleased.

The barrage had moved on to the German rear, and it was impossible to change the plan owing to the very strict and rigid instructions previously laid down. The infantry were left to their fate for the most of the rest of the day.

The advance 'melted away', as the *Official History* puts it, before it ever reached the German lines. The Fourth Division, however, succeeded in crossing the German front trench, suffering terrible loss. It eventually had to retire. 'The extended lines started in excellent order, but gradually melted away. There was no wavering or attempting to come back, the men fell in their ranks – mostly before the first hundred yards of No Man's Land had been crossed.'

Small parties actually succeeded in crossing the first line of defences and even entered Serre. Various observers reported that they saw part of a company of the 11th East Lancashires enter the village, between eight-thirty and nine-fifteen. Some men of the 12th York and Lancasters must have also reached the village, for during another unsuccessful attempt to take place, weeks later, bodies of men of that regiment were found there. All those of both regiments who did reach Serre must have been either killed or taken prisoner within a few hours.

At Corps headquarters, about eight miles behind the line, encouraging reports were received during the morning. But discomfort was felt when it was realized that there was a complete absence of German prisoners coming back to fill the prepared cages. Communications were bad; many senior officers had been killed. Contradictory orders were issued. Artillery fire remained too far ahead and ineffective.

Late in the morning the Corps Commander, Hunter-Weston, realized that the attack was not succeeding. He ordered a new bombardment for twelve o'clock, to last twenty-five minutes.

At twelve-thirty there was to be another attack. It was, however, most difficult to get this instruction forward. There were heavy casualties among runners going forward to the trenches. Remnants of units which had been thrown back from the German line were cluttering up the trenches and causing further confusion. It was difficult to get ammunition up.

Some of the units did not receive the order to attack again until one-thirty. The Seaforth Highlanders never received it at all, and the Dublin Fusiliers lost so heavily that it was impossible to reorganize them.

At the end of the day VIII Corps was back in its trenches, bloody, exhausted and beaten. It had nothing at all to show for over thirteen thousand casualties.

Next to the VIII Corps was the X Corps. The line here was broken by the River Ancre, which ran straight across from the German to the British lines. Below the Ancre were Thiepval and the Leipzig Salient. The second and third system of trenches here were as strong or stronger than the first, consisting of such fortifications on high points as the 'Wonder Work', the Schwaben Redoubt, and the village of St. Pierre Divion which defended the marshy banks of the Ancre. All along the front line there were spurs and re-entrants, providing deadly crossfire against the attacker.

At seven-thirty it was the same story here as on the northern part of the front. Men were mown down everywhere by machine-guns that were able to operate unopposed. Isolated parties broke through, but communications and supplies of reinforcements and ammunition broke down. The village of Thiepval, heavily fortified, although laid level by the preliminary bombardment, was never taken. But the Corps Headquarters thought it had fallen, and it went unmolested from the British artillery throughout the day. Part of one division in the corps, however, had a different story.

The 36th Division (Ulster) recorded one of the most remarkable feats of the whole day in this battle of flesh against bullets.

Some of the battalions had crept forward before zero, and lay as close as a hundred yards before the German line. At seven-thirty the bugles sounded; the Irishmen rose up, and marched forward as though on parade, heavily supported by more battalions behind. The forward troops reached the German trenches before the defenders, who had rushed up from their shelters as soon as the barrage lifted, were fully prepared or had their machine-guns in position. The front trenches were taken with comparatively little loss. The Division went on, neglecting to deal with many Germans still left in the deep dug-outs. It advanced up to three miles, and reached places that were not trodden on again by British troops for two and a half months.

The Ulster Division was different from all other divisions of the British Army. For strength of ties, close blood relationships, and common interests it was unique. Every man in it was Protestant and a Unionist. It was stated by an observer at the time that it was unparalleled since Cromwell's 'Ironsides' in enlisting religious favour and political unity in a military force. One of the sergeants in the Inniskillings wore his orange sash, and many men wore orange ribbons. Shouting 'Remember the Boyne' and 'No surrender, boys' (the legendary answer given by the defenders of Derry to the Jacobites), they carried out one of the most courageous infantry advances, in the face of a wall of bullets, in modern fighting. But as they overran one line of German trenches after another, the Division rapidly diminished in numbers. 'It was like playing leapfrog with death,' as one of them put it. Four V.C.s were awarded to the Division on 1 July.

Casualties were mounting up; the enemy were beginning to organize counter-attacks. Units were splitting up and intermingling. Communications with the rear were bad. Suddenly new orders, on the spot, were needed if the Ulstermen were to keep the extraordinary initiative they had gained.

But the commander of the Ulster Division had ordered all commanding officers to remain behind and not accompany the attacking battalions. Their lives were too valuable. At the critical moment, therefore, a sense of direction was lost, and the Division paid for it.

As has already been related two officers disobeyed this order; one was killed, the other, F. P. Crozier, survived to tell the tale:

As had been surmised by us, neither the fortified Thiepval, nor the strongly fortified Beaumont Hamel, fell. Colonel Bernard was killed at the head of his battalion by trench-mortar fire from the village, which also wiped out his two leading companies following behind him in columns of four. That plan was the plan of the higher hierarchy – not of the fighting front.

Observing what was happening to Bernard 500 yards away on my right, I was driven to alter, by word of mouth above the din, the mode of my deployment. The deployment was accomplished – but, of course, had I been obeying orders in my dug-out no such alteration could have been ordered. The four company commanders would have thought and acted in four different ways. The alteration meant that instead of losing everybody in the first five minutes, we lost only about fifty men.

Crozier went over to Bernard's battalion to see if proper command had been restored; he found that it had not.

Withdrawing my revolver from its holster, I called upon Bernard's remnants to follow me to the front line, a distance of about 300 yards. Not a man moved. I told them I would shoot ... had I been unarmed, and told these men to go forward, I very much doubt if any notice would have taken of me.

The disobeying of an order, at the wise suggestion of Colonel Bernard, who paid for it with his life, surmounted by the fact that his men got there, enabled the Ulster Division to claim justly that it had carried all before it and fulfilled its task.

The true story could not be written at the time in the reports and war diaries, for the simple reason that despite the obvious desirability of officers being permitted to break orders in certain circumstances and despite the absurdity of an army commander being able to dictate to a battalion commander his conduct during battle, if we had told the whole truth we might all have got into trouble.

The Division, despite its momentary success, was now exposed on both flanks, as the attacks on either side had failed, and also German posts which had been overrun too casually were now active again. Reserves did not appear, owing to confusion at the rear. Neither divisional nor corps H.Q. had a clear idea as to what was happening. Many of the Ulstermen were killed or captured before they returned under fire, many of them in rags, to their original trenches. They were confused. They thought they had won a costly victory. But it had turned out something like defeat. There is bad feeling about this in Ulster to this day, many survivors believing they were let down by English divisions on their flanks. Of the over nine thousand casualties of the X Corps, more than half of them were in the Ulster Division. It had been the original Anniversary of the Battle of the Boyne. Eleven days later there was a five minutes' silence in Belfast, in which every machine and movement was stilled. 1 July is still a day of deep mourning in Ulster.

South of the X Corps was the III Corps. It faced two spurs, bulging out in front of the villages of Ovillers and La Boisselle. Between the spurs ran two re-entrants; Sausage Valley and Mash Valley. Opposite La Boisselle the distance between British and German trenches was only fifty yards (the British section being known as the 'Glory Hole'). Any advance was bound to meet crossfire, no matter from what direction it was planned. The faultiness of the ammunition in the preliminary artillery barrage was particularly severe here; there were numerous premature bursts, falling short of shells, and unexploded shells.

Within ten minutes of zero, eighty per cent of the leading battalions were casualties. The Germans here had been well warned of the attack, and a few seconds after zero had complete mastery of No Man's Land. Over most of the front, despite continuous efforts throughout the morning and afternoon, few men reached the German forward trench. Those that did were hopelessly cut off as they disappeared up Sausage and Mash. A fresh reserve brigade was brought up ready to go to their rescue, but by late afternoon, all signs of fighting along the German line having ceased, the attack was called off.

Here are the losses of some of the battalions: 2nd Middlesex, 22 officers and 592 other ranks; 8th York and Lancaster, 23 officers and 613 men; 9th York and Lancaster, 23 officers and 517 men.

In little more than two hours the 8th Division lost 218 out of 300 officers, and 5,274 out of 8,500 other ranks who had gone into action. The German battalions opposite lost 8 officers and 273 men. A reserve battalion had been standing by, but it had not been thought necessary to call upon it.

The XV Corps recorded the first meagre successes of the day. Here again the corps faced a large salient. There were two fortified villages (a strong-house in one of them had four-inch steel armour): Fricourt, which came up right behind the German front trench; and Mametz, which was half a mile to the rear.

No Man's Land was narrow on parts of this front, and this

enabled some of the attacking troops to get a foothold on the forward trenches before they had all been annihilated coming across. Machine-gun strength here was exceptionally strong, some of the crews continuing to fire when hopelessly surrounded, when they were shot at point blank range. One gunner was found chained to his weapon, whether by himself or others it was never discovered.

Some advance to both sides of Fricourt was made and held throughout the day, reinforcements being brought up, and considerable numbers of Germans were taken prisoner. Mametz was first entered by a few survivors of the 1st South Staffordshires as early as eight o'clock. By three o'clock the village was in British hands, its ruins littered with dead and dying British soldiers.

Fricourt, in the centre of the XV Corps front, however, remained impregnable, despite being completely outflanked. The 7th Green Howards, 10th West Yorkshires, and 7th East Yorkshires all vainly tried to storm this strong-point, bristling with machine-guns. The West Yorkshires were annihilated. The Green Howards were only three companies strong, one company having attacked at the wrong time; both these battalions were practically wiped out within three minutes by a single well-placed machine-gun. A few men reached the village, only to be slaughtered (although one little group hid in a cellar and survived).

By nightfall Fricourt was still held by Germans, but the XV Corps had advanced over three-quarters of a mile to either side of the village, and had taken Mametz. It lost over eight thousand casualties, almost entirely due to machine-gun fire.

On the right flank of the British line, next to the French, the southernmost corps of the Fourth Army, the XIII, recorded better successes than the XV. Artillery fire here had been very great, and apparently more successful than elsewhere. Parts of the German trench system had been completely levelled; the village of Montauban had been destroyed and a large brickworks near by had been reduced to a pile of rubble. The artillery had a greater advantage than elsewhere, out-numbering the German guns by at least four to one, and during the opening of the attack the British troops were able to move about with an almost complete absence of enemy fire (other corps suffered heavily during 1 July from artillery fire on reserves and communications). A good deal of this successful bombardment was from the French batteries to the south. The German troops here were more demoralized from the barrage than elsewhere, this being added to by the fact that they had not received proper rations during the six days of the bombardment. Parts of the first trench were overrun with little resistance; at other places lone machine-guns held out, causing as always, heavy casualties.

There had been some very successful tunnelling by the XIII Corps engineers across No Man's Land. Six tunnels had been dug, with only a small charge being detonated at zero to give entry to German dug-outs and trenches. Also the wire here had been better cut by the artillery.

One division, the 30th, attained its objective in little over an hour. The second line of the first system of trenches was more sternly defended, although Montauban itself was entered by Manchesters and Scots Fusiliers at five past ten, the only living thing discovered there being a terrified fox. A whole French battery had fired on the village ceaselessly for seven days.

At night, fighting ceased, and the XIII Corps was able to congratulate itself that it was the most successful of the British corps engaged on the first day of the Battle of the Somme. At one point it had advanced well over a mile from its line, suffering six thousand casualties in doing so. Such were the wretched results elsewhere that this was later to be considered a great success.

That night, down the whole line, men were busy clearing up the mess of disaster. Brigades were being assembled, men counted, communications renewed, water, food, and ammunition brought up to the forward positions, new trenches dug. All this was hampered by the fact that the British front trenches, which were now mostly the front line once more, were cluttered up with dead, dying, and wounded.

Towards the south of the line hardly a shot was fired by the enemy after dark, as he too was busy reorganizing, and the work could proceed unhindered by artillery fire. At several places there was a shortage of water, the demand being greater than expected, and many men went without food.

Now also the task of collecting the shattered soldiers who had been lying all day in No Man's Land was begun. Because of the enormous numbers of wounded, the stretcher bearers were unable to cope with the job alone, and large numbers of artillery, engineers, and pioneers were called in to help during the night. Due to the shortage of stretchers, blankets were used. On the whole the Germans did not molest these operations, although there were a few incidents, due mainly to misunderstandings.

Opposite Allenby's VII Corps the Germans hoisted a large red cross flag while the wounded were brought in. There was ceremonial saluting on both sides. Two days later a German plane dropped a list of prisoners taken at Gommecourt, and the courtesy was returned by the same means.

During the night there was a continual coming and going of men, as desperate efforts were made to sort out the chaos many units had got into. To the north of the line, there was some heavy artillery fire from the enemy. The line was straightened, and wire was laid, or relaid. The night sky was full of flashes, and star shells rose, poised and then floated down. Dull explosions sounded all the time. In Amiens (twenty miles away) people got out of their beds to see the flashes and hear the distant roar of the guns. Even this far away, windows had been trembling for the past week.

Across No Man's Land, in the fine, summer night air, Germans were, in places, busying themselves digging graves and marking crosses: 'To a Brave Englander' or 'To Brave English Soldiers'.

Meanwhile the Ulstermen who had gone so far and so well during the day were falling back to the British line in confusion. Completely disillusioned, nothing could stop them. Colonel Crozier, still with what remained of his Belfast battalion of the Royal Irish Rifles, wrote:

> The line broke at the Schwaben Redoubt and men in the dark mixed up with other units of the division, and units of a reinforcing division, were hurled back in a rabble, clothes in tatters, rifles discarded or left lying on the ground; there was some shooting [of men by their own officers].

One officer told Crozier,

> how, in desperation, he fired his revolver into a crowd of British soldiers on the run, hoping to stop them without having an idea who they were or to which units they belonged.

But such tactics were to no avail. The men of Ulster had had enough for one day. We can leave Crozier as he smokes a cigarette and surveys the scene in the first dim light of dawn.

'The birds have gone, nature has been supplanted. The wood itself has disappeared.'

At Fourth Army H.Q. the exact result of the battle was still not clear. The last Fourth Army report issued at six fifty p.m. stated that two battalions were believed to be holding Serre. As we have seen, only a handful of men reached the village and had been killed hours before. Rawlinson had spent the day in his room at Army H.Q., talking on the telephone to his corps commanders who knew little more than he did. Even quite late reports continued to be encouraging, although verbal ones were, it seems, less so than those which had to be written. Says the *Official History:* 'No thought of failure had entered anyone's head.'

Haig told Rawlinson that he wished the attack to be continued the next day, and at ten p.m. Fourth Army issued an order to all corps to 'continue the attack'. A solid footing was still required in the German first line. The new attacks were to be made 'under corps arrangements as early as possible'.

The two northerly corps, the X and VIII, were to be placed under the command of General Gough, as Haig thought, rightly, that Rawlinson would have enough to do to reorganize the remainder, and exploit the success of XIII Corps. This was, in fact, done at Rawlinson's suggestion. Gough at once left his cavalry division to visit the new command, which was to become the Fifth Army, to 'ascertain their situation and condition', a task which should not have taken him long.

The day was nearly over, and soldiers sat down, after one of the bloodiest episodes in history, to write in their diaries before going to get what sleep they could.

At nine thirty Siegfried Sassoon wrote:

C Company now reduced to six runners, two stretcher-bearers, Company Sergeant-Major, signallers, and Barton's servant. Sky cloudy westward. Red sunset. Heavy gun-fire on the left.

At ten o'clock General Rawlinson wrote:

Not much change in the general situation, but I have put Goughy in command of the two northern corps to co-ordinate their efforts, and see if he cannot push them on again. The casualties to date are 16,000. [They were, in fact, sixty thousand.]

Sir Douglas Haig wrote about the failure of the VIII Corps in its task of assailing an almost impregnable position:

> North of the Ancre, the VIII Corps (Hunter-Weston) said said they began well, but as the day progressed, their troops were forced back into the German front line [in fact few of them reached it in the first place], except two battalions which occupied Serre Village ... I am inclined to believe from further reports, that few of the VIII Corps left their [own] trenches.

The VIII Corps had suffered thirteen thousand casualties carrying out Haig's orders to the best of its ability. Haig continued, writing now of Allenby's VII Corps:

> The attack on Gommecourt salient started well. This attack was of the greatest assistance in helping VIII Corps, because many of the enemy's guns and troops were employed against it, and so the VIII Corps was left considerably free. In spite of this, the VIII Corps achieved very little.

This irritable outburst against Hunter-Weston, whom Haig disliked personally, was almost his last entry for the day. He shows no awe at the large casualty figures beginning by now to come in, nor does he seem to feel than any lack of success might be due to his own failings.

Lieutenant M. St. Helier Evans, who was in reserve, wrote:

> The greatest battle of all time began yesterday. I can vouch for the magnificent organisation leading up to this attack. If we don't get to Bapaume now we never shall. Bapaume is our objective and it is said H.Q. and billets have been mapped out there for us. We have on our side half a million men and the cavalry stands by to ride through. The death roll is not as great as was expected. It is felt we shall get through this time and end stagnant warfare.

King Albert of the Belgians, with his army away to the north, wrote in his diary:

> French and English together announce 11,000 prisoners. The first German line was captured but we were halted by the second. We are assured that the attackers' losses were negligible, naturally! Now we are marking time and bringing up artillery; then the attack will continue, and in this way the Germans will have time to bring up their reserves.

In any case no surprise effect has been sought. This is a sledge-hammer attack, not a penetration. Penetration is antiquated! In any case this offensive, by wearing down the armies taking part, is leading us towards the end of the war. When this battle has lasted two or three months weariness may set in and ideas of peace will at last find favourable soil.

The Battle of the Somme had failed miserably. A glorious victory had been expected; a horrible blood-bath had occurred.

A most unsuitable place had been selected for the attack. Preparations were not fully carried out, owing to the urgent appeals of the French – in six weeks' time the number of reserves would have been considerably larger. The chance of surprise that an attack in early morning mist, before the deadly machine-gunners could see far, had been lost by Douglas Haig giving in to the French on the lateness of zero hour. There were not enough heavy howitzers. The barrage had not had the effect of destroying the German resistance and wire, owing to the depth of the dug-outs unknown to or unreported by British intelligence. Only on the southern, Montauban, front were the dug-outs found to be affected by artillery fire. Much of the ammunition had been faulty.

Infantry had not been able to walk across No Man's Land and take possession of the enemy ground; they had been overloaded and provided sitting targets. The N.C.O.s of the new army had been inexperienced and knew little more than their private soldiers. And N.C.O.s are the backbone of infantry. Out-of-date tactical formations had been used. Reserves had been marched up in columns of four when machine-guns were still active in the area. No attempts at concealment, surprise, initiative, or flexibility were called for; and with very few exceptions were not made.

Nothing had been left to the discretion of local commanders. Instructions were rigid, and were often adhered to even when obviously futile. A number of units had succeeded in breaking through, but had received no support on their flanks. Artillery fire was poured down far behind the enemy line, leaving the German defending infantry unscathed even after the initial assault had failed. Both communications and supplies broke down.

The attack, instead of being called off, as many survivors fully expected it to be, was on the contrary to be continued immediately. A catastrophe had occurred, but the only people who could stop it recurring were the very ones who did not, or would not, realize it. Thus ended the most costly day the British Army has ever known. The first official figure was 61,816 casualties; this was later reduced to 57,470, it being stated that many of the missing later rejoined. The reduction of seven per cent is certainly too high. The true figure is probably very close to sixty thousand, of whom about a third were presumably killed (the official figure for killed or died of wounds is 19,240). Gough himself gives them as 60,695.

Just behind the line, all day, the cavalry had waited. Horses had whinnied and stamped. Troopers had smoked and nervously calmed their steeds. In leafy lanes and farm courtyards three divisions of spotless, beautifully groomed cavalry had waited for the gap through which they were to charge and sabre the enemy guns.

CHAPTER THIRTEEN

THE FRENCH

THE part the French played in the Battle of the Somme should not be underrated. In fact, on 1 July, they attacked on a front of nearly eight miles (compared with the British eighteen) with three corps (a total of five divisions). And in the end they advanced on a broader front than did the British. This book, however, is primarily concerned with the British effort and will not examine the French actions during the summer, autumn, and winter in detail.

The French Sixth Army commander, Fayolle, was an intelligent soldier, and he had at his disposal fifty thousand of the best infantry in France. These consisted of the XX Corps (the famous 'Iron Corps'), which had won a great tradition under its original commander, Foch; the XXXV Corps; and the I Colonial Corps, which was made up of notoriously fiery and fierce colonial troops. British observers were startled to come across lone Arab horsemen, carefully picking their way through the debris. The Iron Corps was one of the best known military units of the whole war. It had saved the day at Nancy in 1914, and turned the tide at Verdun on the critical 26 February 1916. It was the flower of the French shock troops, full of experienced, tough infantrymen, who had learned how and when to cross No Man's Land.

Fayolle's army was under the control of Foch, who commanded the northern sector of the French front. Foch was a wily, elderly (even for the French) General who desperately wanted to prove himself and help save France from the agony of Verdun. He was due to reach retirement age in a few weeks.

The French preparations had been better than the British. There had been a greater concentration of supplies. Artillery had been much heavier and more accurate. They had 850 heavy guns and were even able to lend Rawlinson a hundred. Fayolle's chief of staff, Colonel Duval, was an outstanding soldier; among other innovations, he insisted on a conference each night of all corps chiefs of staff.

Although the Germans were suspicious of French intentions on the Somme, especially when they noticed a troop build-up from 24 May, they made their main preparations opposite the British lines. They believed it possible that, owing to Verdun, any projected French attack might not materialize.

The French line actually bestrode the Somme, which was wide and marshy where it crossed the line. North of it was the XX Corps, between the river and the British XIII Corps. South of it were the other two corps, with another in reserve. Unlike the British sector, the line was almost entirely straight, the only small indentation being a French salient, which was to their advantage. The French seemed to have known what they were doing when, the year before, they had asked the British to take over the sector north of the Somme which turned out to be a tactical paradise for the Germans.

The Iron Corps attacked north of the river at seven thirty, the same time as the British. They were greatly helped by a river mist which enabled them to move a good way across No Man's Land unobserved. By midday the situation was so good, all objectives having been taken, that the local commander was anxious to push on, with every likelihood of making a real gap in the German line. He had, however, to be withheld owing to the static state of his left flank, the British XIII Corps. The official French report stated that by nightfall the XX Corps was 'in occupation of the entire German first position; it had suffered very few losses and had not employed any reserves, not even partially'.

South of the river the attack did not take place till nine thirty. This was an idea of Foch's, who realized, rightly, that it would cause complete surprise. By eight thirty the Germans opposite had given up all idea of a French attack, thinking the battle was going to be confined to the north of the river. Most of the German line was overrun, and by evening the advance had gone about half a mile farther than expected, and the German second system was in danger.

All this had been achieved through the well-tried military principle of surprise, now out of fashion with the British; by the fact that the troops were experienced and well trained; by the greater elasticity allowed to both local infantry and artillery officers (in some places attacks were delayed until junior officers were satisfied that the barrage had done its work); and to the more effective barrage itself. The Colonial Corps, for instance, had about three times as much artillery as any British corps possessed.

With all their objectives achieved or bettered with few casualties, the French showed on 1 July that there could be such a thing as sophistication and efficiency in trench warfare; and that the British still had a lot to learn if the war was, indeed, to be won that way. They took four thousand prisoners and lost hardly any themselves. The following day they could have advanced much farther and there is no doubt that the German line could have been completely sundered by the French at the Somme. But they were continually hampered by their left flank and the possibility of exposing it. They were not themselves strong enough to reach a decision; and something seemed to have gone very wrong with the British Army and its command. The French settled down to a weary battle of attrition, which might have frustrated Foch, but certainly did not displease General Joffre.

On 11 July, the Germans made their last attack at Verdun. On 15 July the French assumed the offensive. They soon started to recapture much of the few thousand yards of precious, but churned-up, French soil they had lost. In all, there were nearly half a million French casualties at Verdun. An enormous, bitter, and bloody battle had been fought. A battle that would have little, if any, effect on the final result of the war; that had only succeeded in making sure another battle, more bloody still, would follow it, which might otherwise have been prevented, or at least postponed until the attackers were better prepared to undertake it. So the inevitable aspect of the Western Front rolled on its way, with horrors looming up every day that men seemed unable to stop.

But General Joffre, at least, was able to resume his former composure, which, with his public reputation, he had been in danger of losing altogether. Despite the distrust of the politicians in Paris, who knew him better than did the public, he seemed safe for a while longer. France had won a great victory at Verdun, or so the authorities said.

CHAPTER FOURTEEN

'ACROSS NO MAN'S LAND

THE British bombardment had caused heavy damage to the German front trenches although practically none at all to the dug-outs. When their troops rushed out of the shelters just after seven thirty on 1 July, many who had been below for several days were amazed at the state to which their defences had been reduced. In some places there was only a string of craters – these, however, afforded excellent cover and vantage points for the machine-gunners.

At the south of the line, opposite the French and the XIII Corps, the barrage had also affected the dug-outs. And here the men were so demoralized and their collapse so sudden that clerks, cooks, batmen and other odd-job men were rounded up to occupy the second position.

At least one dug-out was covered up by a shell bursting near its entrance, and the occupants had to wait all day before they were released. At other places they remained down of their own volition, and spent the battle in some comfort, and at others they emerged after the British had passed over them, to attack from the rear.

But on the whole, once the barrage on the front had ceased, the Germans did not have an uncomfortable time. Most of von Below's six divisions were unembarrassed by the efforts of the nineteen allied divisions hurled against them. About a hundred machine-gun crews had done the real work, but riflemen also were able to stand up and shoot at will, the British infantrymen having little cover from which to fire, and the New Army soldiers being bad shots (a part of their training which had been seriously neglected).

A German eye-witness, quoted by Churchill, wrote:

The intense bombardment was realised by all to be a prelude to the infantry assault at last. The men in the dug-outs therefore waited ready, a belt full of hand grenades around them, gripping their rifles and listening for the bombardment to lift from the front defence zone on to the rear defences. It was of vital importance to lose not a second in taking up position in the open to meet the British infantry. Looking towards the British trenches, through the long trench periscopes held up out of the dug-out entrances, there could be seen a mass of steel helmets above their parapet showing that their storm-troops were ready for the assault. At 7.30 a.m. the hurricane of shells ceased as suddenly as it had begun. Our men at once clambered up the steep shafts leading from the dug-outs to daylight and ran for the nearest shell craters. The machine-guns were pulled out of the dug-outs and hurriedly placed into position, their crews dragging the heavy ammunition boxes up the steps and out to the guns. A rough firing line was thus rapidly established. As soon as in position, a series of extended lines of British infantry were seen moving forward from the British trenches. The first line appeared to continue without end to right and left. It was quickly followed by a second line, then a third and fourth. They came on at a steady easy pace as if expecting to find nothing alive in our front trenches ... The front line, preceded by a thin line of skirmishers and bombers, was now half-way across No Man's Land. 'Get ready!' was passed along our front from crater to crater, and heads appeared over the crater edges as final positions were taken up for the best view and machine-guns mounted firmly in place. A few minutes later, when the leading British line was within 100 yards, the rattle of machine-gun and rifle fire broke out from along the whole line of craters. Some fired kneeling so as to get a better target over the broken ground, while others in the excitement of the moment stood up, regardless of their own safety, to fire into the crowd of men in front of them. The advance rapidly crumpled under this hail of shells and bullets. All along the line men could be seen throwing their arms into the air and collapsing never to move again. Badly wounded rolled about in their agony, and others less severely injured crawled to the nearest shell hole. The noise of the battle became indescribable. The shouting of orders and the shrill British cheers as they charged forward could be heard above the violent and intense fusillade of machine-guns and rifles and the bursting bombs, and above the deep thundering of the artillery and the shell explosions. With all this were mingled the moans and groans of the wounded, the cries for help and the last screams of death. Again and again the extended lines of British infantry broke against the German defence like waves against a cliff, only to be beaten back. It was an amazing spectacle of unexampled gallantry, courage and bull-dog determination on both sides.

The delay of fire was described in this account was quite unusual on 1 July, many of the German machine-gunners opening fire immediately they got their guns facing across No Man's Land.

The German official history speaks of 'the wonderful effect of the machine-guns'. It describes one British brigade as advancing in 'solid lines without gaps in faultless order, led by its officers carrying battle flags and sticks. Wave after wave was shot down by well-aimed fire ... a wall of dead British was piled up on the front.'

There was some confusion behind the German lines, due to the barrage, and the badly organized system of commands. A counter-attack on one part of the front, ordered as early as five past eight, did not take place till one o'clock. Communications were suffering nearly as badly as behind the British lines.

German intransigence was largely due to the strict ideas of Falkenhayn. In common with the allied commanders, he preferred to lose men rather than a yard or two of ground. He had von Below's chief-of-staff replaced for allowing a German corps to withdraw before French pressure on 2 July. And he issued an order: 'Not a foot of ground must be voluntarily abandoned. Only over our dead bodies will the enemy advance.'

And so the irresistible force was pitted against the immovable object.

CHAPTER FIFTEEN

'CARRY ON!'

As the full meaning of the disaster on the day before began to reach Haig on 2 July, his plan for the continuation of the attack (there is nothing on record to suggest that he considered calling it off) began to take shape. There were reserves of men to fill the gaps in the ranks, although the full extent of the losses was still not yet known, but there was a serious shortage of artillery ammunition. The two northern corps, now under Gough, were ordered to stand fast, reorganize, and consider new plans; in the south, where there had been some advance towards Longueval, the attack was to continue. In this way, ammunition supplies could be more or less concentrated in one place.

A policy of 'nibbling' at the German line was prescribed for the southern sector. But as none of the lessons of 1 July had been learnt, and as the assaults continued in disastrous monotony, day after day, thousands of men dying in the process, very little ground was in fact captured during the next two weeks.

July 2 was probably the only day in the whole battle, the Germans being disorganized and in the process of recuperation, when a break-through might have been achieved. That chance was lost, and it never returned again. The Fourth Army had been so mauled that it could not take part in a large-scale effort again for weeks.

On 2 July the rubble of bricks known as Fricourt was taken without any fighting; only eleven German stragglers being found there. On the 3rd, an attack was made on Ovillers, one of the fortified spurs; men of five battalions actually entered the position, but very few returned. Their supply of grenades ran out, it was impossible to send up reserves, and they were annihilated. Two thousand four hundred men were lost. It was the same story all over again. Says the *Official History*:

The action was another reminder that an assault on a narrow front, without adequate flank protection and lacking the element of surprise, was bound to result in a useless waste of life. For the infantry to have reached the German trenches at all was an outstanding feat of arms.

The effect of yet another failure on G.H.Q. was to order further similar attacks.

At 3 p.m. on the 3rd, Joffre and Foch came to see Haig to discuss future arrangements. Joffre wanted Haig to attack farther north, around Pozières and Thiepval, which had seen such terrible slaughter forty-eight hours previously. Haig explained his plan of taking advantage of the slight advance farther south, and he asked if the French forces adjoining his line there would co-operate in further combined attacks.

Haig wrote in his diary:

At this, General Joffre exploded in a fit of rage. He could not approve of it. He 'ordered' me to attack Thiepval and Pozières. If I attacked Longueval I would be beaten, etc., etc. I waited calmly till he had finished. His breast heaved and his face flushed! The truth is the poor man cannot argue, nor can he easily read a map. When Joffre got out of breath, I quietly explained what my position is relatively to him as the 'Generalissimo'. I am solely responsible to the British Government for the action of the British army; and I had approved the plan, and must modify it to suit the changing situation as the fight progresses. I was most polite. Joffre saw he had made a mistake, and next tried to cajole me. He said that this was the 'English Battle' and 'France expected great things from me.'

At length, Haig's views were accepted by Joffre, and he had some justification for his self-satisfied little note. This was the first major occasion when he stood up to Joffre's bullying and had not been swayed by it. The pity is that he had not done so long before.

Haig, however, did not seem to realize the full implication of Joffre's temper, almost certainly simulated. Joffre was able to read a map only too well. One of the reasons he had picked this part of the Western Front for the battles was because he knew that a battle of attrition was likely to result. He knew that the Thiepval sector was about the strongest part of the German line at the Somme, and foresaw a long and bloody battle there – just the thing to help relieve Verdun, and give the French breathing time.

Foch felt unable to help the British intentions on the Longueval front for the time being, although he agreed to continue to provide artillery support.

And so the 'nibbling' continued. Every wood, every farmhouse, every windmill, which were only fictions on the maps and figments of the minds of staff officers who had never seen the front, had to be taken separately, sometimes with ten thousand men or more. Heavy showers began on 7 July, turning much of the shelled and churned-up ground into a quagmire. Trenches were knee-deep, in some places waist-deep, in slime, and under shell-fire disappeared altogether. Says the *Official History*: 'Movement was often agony: men fainted from sheer exhaustion while struggling through deep mud; in some localities a team of 14 horses were required to bring up a single ammunition wagon.' Altogether the rain only lasted two days, chaos had appeared. Cases of 'trench feet', a repellent sickness, had already occurred and pessimists began wondering what this ground was going to be like in the winter, if it was still being fought on then.

Attacks were launched again and again on Ovillers and La Boiselle, both heaps of ruin. There was almost no sign at these fortresses of German works, making the task of the attackers all the more difficult. There were strongholds under the ruins, with tiny machine-gun openings. Below were tunnels, well supplied with ammunition and food, and there was access to underground wells for water. The defenders had orders to fight to the death, and even when surrounded they continued to do so; some witnesses consider the fighting here was the bloodiest of the whole war. Men crawled up the sides of the hills, groping about in search of the German fortresses. Often the first sign that they had reached their objective was their own slaughter. Being on spurs about six hundred yards apart, they were able to supply crossfire and covering fire for each other (Ovillers was eventually taken on the 17th, and according to C. E. Montague in *Disenchantment* a piece of paper was found there with the British orders written on it, word for word, for the first assault. La Boiselle was taken earlier – when arms were presented by British troops as the starving survivors emerged.)

Behind the line there was an indescribable mess of destruction in what had been No Man's Land and the old German front line. M. St. Helier Evans described it in his diary: 'The whole area is littered with debris, equipment soaked in blood, discarded weapons and all the aftermath of fierce scrapping.

Every yard is pitted with shell-holes.' Looting was going on full scale (prisoners as well as the dead being considered fair game). German prisoners were observed with curiosity; 'the enemy come in very grimy, many are bearded and many wear large specs. or pincenez. Their blue-grey uniform shows up more than our colour. One man bore a label "Wanted by G.H.Q." '

Men lined up for their tots of rum. The Royal Welch Fusiliers put on a concert with a cart as a stage. Divisional bands played martial music beside where the great masses of reserves were camped, waiting to go up to the line. 'The adjutant saw me about accumulated allowances,' wrote Evans. 'I told him not to bother, it seems so trivial.'

Siegfried Sassoon was also behind the line. 'There was much battle gear lying about, and some dead horses. There were rags and shreds of clothing, boots riddled and torn, and when we came to the old German front line a sour pervasive stench which differed from anything my nostrils had known before.'

Sassoon met his friend Robert Graves, who was with a reserve brigade. (Poets present on the Somme, in one capacity or another, included Graves, Sassoon, Mark Plowman, David Jones, Edmund Blunden, and John Masefield.) He, too, was horrified by the scene of desolation in the battleground on 1 July. He wrote: 'I came across two unforgettable corpses: a man of the South Wales Borderers and one of the Lehr Regiment had succeeded in bayoneting each other simultaneously.'

One of the most typical of the engagements taking place at this time was the struggle for the wood at Mametz, in which the British made almost as many difficulties for themselves as they received from the Germans. It was a thick wood, of hornbeams, limes, oaks, and a few beeches. The undergrowth was high, and there was much bramble. German machine-gunners and snipers had made some use of camouflage, and severe wire entanglements were knitted with the undergrowth. The way in which the British went about taking this wood, which was not in fact very heavily held, was clumsy in the extreme. The bombardment had made the wood, on a spur and with an area of about two hundred acres, into even more of a maze. It was continually full of smoke, and sometimes partly on fire. Haig himself was particularly concerned with its capture. Rawlinson, however, told him that some of the senior commanders would have to be relieved of their commands before a successful assault on the wood could be launched. This was done.

On 8 July, a corps order was issued at 1.40 p.m., directing the 38th Division to secure part of Mametz Wood. Reports were coming in that it was deserted (but other reports stated that patrols had been fired on when approaching it). Division ordered brigade to carry out the attack. Brigade ordered a battalion (the 14th Welch Fusiliers). Battalion ordered a platoon. The platoon commander, however, had to report that owing to confusion in the trenches, his platoon had found it impossible to reach the starting point of the attack. Mametz Wood was not taken that night; nor was it to be taken so casually.

Another attack was ordered for the 10th – but on this occasion the whole division was to take part. Sassoon was concerned with one of the previous small-scale attempts on the wood. He describes one expedition.

It had lasted nearly eleven hours and we had walked less than three miles, which was about all that we congratulate ourselves on. From a military point of view the operation had enabled the Staff to discover that Mametz Wood was still full of Germans so that it was impossible to dig a trench on the bluff within 50 yards of it, as had been suggested. It was obvious now that a few strong patrols could have clarified the situation more economically than 1,000 men with picks and shovels.

A few days later Sassoon (known as 'Mad Jack') succeeded in capturing a trench single-handed just outside the wood, whereupon, according to Robert Graves,

he sat down in the German trench and began reading a book of poems which he had brought with him. When he finally went back he did not even report. The attack on Mametz Wood had been delayed for two hours because British patrols were still reported to be out. 'British patrols' were Siegfried and his book of poems.

Sassoon eventually got into the wood.

Our men seemed a bit out of hand and I couldn't see any of the responsible N.C.O.s ... Along [a] path came someone in a hurry. He bumped into me and I flashed the torch on his face. He was an officer who had joined us the week before. He had now lost all control of himself and I gathered from

his incoherent utterances that he was on his way to Headquarters to tell them that his Company hadn't moved yet
because they didn't know which way to go to find the Germans.

To receive their instructions for the 10th, brigadiers had to
trek to divisional headquarters, six miles behind the line. So
it was nearly midnight when battalions got their orders for
the attack the following day. Troops had to cover a thousand
yards of open ground before they reached the edge of the
wood, and nearly all this was uphill. The attack took place
in early daylight and was immediately machine-gunned and
decimated. Officers took over the groups nearest at hand. The
British barrage was short and many men were killed by their
own guns. The edge of the wood was reached by some units,
which took shelter there.

Patrols of the advanced units delved into the wood and
reported the enemy was not there in great numbers. At some
parts opposition ceased, and two battalion commanders asked
for permission to go on. A further artillery barrage of the
wood, however, had been arranged and it was found impossible to alter this. After a respite, the enemy thought better
of evacuating the wood. Shelling had made the scene into a
nightmare landscape. One who was there wrote: 'Limbs and
mutilated trunks, here and there a detached head, forming
splashes of red against the green leaves ... one tree held in
its branches a leg, with its torn flesh hanging down over a spray
of leaf.' Swarms of flies, blackening the corpses, revolted many
more than anything else they saw.

When the second stage of the advance did at last take place,
there was much wild shooting in the trees, and dreadful confusion. Telephone wires had been cut by enemy artillery or by
British shells falling short, and practically all the runners were
casualties (in one brigade all ninety-six of them were lost).
Attempts to reorganize the confused mass of troops inside the
wood were unsuccessful.

Eventually, however, it was cleared to within forty yards
of its northern edge. A decision for another attack, to clear it
completely, was cancelled owing to the exhaustion of the
troops. Mametz Wood was now ceaselessly shelled, the crack-
ing of the wood and the explosions making a deafening noise,
and there was some panicking.

Next day another brigade relieved that which had spent a

day and night fighting in Mametz Wood, and it was ordered to attack. After a personal reconnaissance (in which he and his staff were wounded) the brigadier advised against the attack. In reply he was directed to clear the wood of Germans immediately. After considerable losses the task was eventually completed.

This incredible story of bungling is well illustrated by the memories of L. W. Griffith in *Up to Mametz*.

At 8.0 the artillery began its bombardment of the edge of Mametz Wood. A thousand yards away from where I stood our two battalions were waiting. I read the orders again. The attack was to be carried out in three stages beginning at 8.30, reaching in succession three positions inside the wood, under the protection of an artillery barrage. Smoke-screens were to be formed here and there. Everything sounded so simple and easy.

A few minutes after 8.0 all our telephone wires to the battalions were cut by the enemy's reply to our fire. There was no smoke-screen, for some reason never explained — perhaps someone forgot about it. This was the first departure from the simplicity of the printed word. Messages came through, a steady trickle of runners bringing evil news; our fire had not smashed the German machine-guns in Mametz Wood, nor in the wood near Bazentin. The elaborate time-table suddenly became a thing of no meaning, as unrelated to our condition as one of Napoleon's orders.

Griffith, a staff officer, accompanied his brigadier to see the front. The troops were stuck on the slope before the wood, unable to get any farther, with machine-gun fire from the front and the right. Wounded were streaming back. Survivors were trying desperately to dig themselves in to get what cover they could.

'This is sheer lunacy,' said the brigadier. 'I've tried all day to stop it. We could creep up to the edge of the wood by night and rush it in the morning, but they won't listen to me.'

'If I could get you through on the telephone, would you talk to them again?' asked Griffith.

The General said he would, but all the lines were cut. Eventually Griffith found one still intact.

The brigadier told Griffith: 'Difficult to judge on the spot, they said. As good as told me I was tired and didn't want to tackle the job. As if the whole trouble hadn't arisen because someone had found it so easy to judge when he was six miles away.'

Later, in the wood, the brigadier received a staff officer from Army H.Q. He told him that he intended to take the rest of the wood by surprise. He begged him to take the message back, that he did not *want* any artillery barrage. But a barrage was sent nevertheless – right on top of the brigadier's attacking troops.

The brigadier sat down on a tree stump and said: 'This is the end of everything ... sheer stupidity.' Six weeks later he was sent home. (So was the Divisional General; 'broken down in health,' said Lloyd George in a letter to his brother.)

The casualties in the second week of the Somme fighting averaged around ten thousand a day.

The first official report was now sent back to London. It read:

After ten days and nights of continuous fighting, our troops have completed the methodical capture of the whole of the enemy's first system of defence on a front of 14,000 yards. This system of defence consisted of numerous and continuous lines of fire trenches, extending to depths of from 2,000 to 4,000 yards, and included five strongly fortified villages, numerous heavily entrenched woods, and a large number of immensely strong redoubts. The capture of each of these trenches represented an operation of some importance, and the whole of them are now in our hands.

The situation on the rest of the line at the Somme, which had been at a standstill since 1 July, was not detailed in the report.

The Germans, also, were taking stock. Falkenhayn wrote:

If by the evening of the second day of the battle it was quite certain that the break-through planned by the English and the French would not succeed, after the first week the G.H.Q. knew with equal certainty that the enemy would also fail to reach his objective in the nibbling tactics to which he had been compelled to resort after the miscarriage of the break-through.

Hundreds of miles away, fighting on the Eastern Front against the huge, ponderous rabble that was the Russian

Imperial Army, another German general, Hindenburg, was sizing up the opponents that he was soon to meet in the West.

'If,' wrote Hindenburg later, 'our Western adversaries failed to obtain any decisive results in the battles of 1915 to 1917, it must be ascribed to a certain unimaginativeness in their generalship.'

After a fortnight of bloody fighting, the British commanders were now beginning to rack their brains to find an answer to the problem of capturing the German second line, without incurring another disaster like the one that had overtaken them when they attacked the first German position. New ideas were not easy to find on the Western Front in 1916, however, and so they went back to an old one – a simple military idea that had served far greater commanders than they.

Rawlinson and his staff thought of the idea of attacking at night, when the troops would be able to reach quite close to the German lines without being seen. It seemed likely that machine-guns would be less effective in the dark than in broad daylight.

Haig, however, strongly objected to this idea. He considered the troops had not had enough training to enable them to make such a complicated manœuvre in darkness. Rawlinson was ordered to think again, but after another conference with his staff he could only report that they were all still strongly in favour of a night attack.

Haig remained unconvinced, but Rawlinson went on with arrangements on his own. Two days before the attack was due he wrote a private letter to Haig, and his chief-of-staff made an appeal to his opposite number at Haig's H.Q., General Kiggell, on the telephone.

Haig gave in, and at 3.25 a.m. on 14 July the attack was launched in the direction of Trones Wood, Longueval, and the two Bazentin villages, *after only five minutes' bombardment*. Another innovation was the 'creeping barrage' which went forward with the advancing infantry, in strictly timed stages.

Rawlinson had hoped to have French support at the southern end of his line for this attack, but the French decided to remain on the defensive, leaving his right flank dangerously in the air. Their commanders, in any case, thought the whole plan absurd, and gave it no chance of success, despite the enthusiastic assurances of Rawlinson's chief-of-staff.

The assembly of the attacking troops by night, twenty-two thousand of them, was a major feat in itself. Many of them were formed up within five hundred yards of the front German trench, without the Germans suspecting anything unusual. White ropes were run out to the front and the units assembled as if at Aldershot. It was a cloudy, but not very dark summer night. All kinds of obstacles and messes of war had to be crossed. It would have been a difficult operation in peacetime; and only one of the battalions was a regular army one.

In parts the leading British wave reached the German wire before a shot was fired. Five miles of the German second line were taken (although one mile was lost the following day).

The French were astounded. The old-world General commanding their XX Corps, on the British right, General Balfourier, who still wore the Second Empire style of uniform, with wide red trousers, commented: 'Alors, le général Montgomery ne mange pas son chapeau.' This referred to the statement of Rawlinson's chief-of-staff, as to what he would do if the attack failed.

For forty-eight hours before the attack, the French had repeatedly phoned the Fourth Army imploring them not to attack. It was, they said, sheer madness. It was the French who had insisted on a daylight attack on 1 July.

If the success developed on 14 July, Rawlinson had hoped to send three cavalry divisions charging through the enemy lines. He considered this of such importance that he kept two of them under his own personal command. This caused the kind of confusion that might have been expected. The cavalry was to be ready by 4 a.m., but the commander of the Secunderabad Cavalry Brigade, which was to lead the charge, was under the control of two corps, and was himself at an infantry divisional H.Q., with liaison officers at various other H.Q.s. His brigade did not begin to advance until the following evening.

While the infantry was waiting for the rest of the cavalry to appear, after the initial success in the early hours of the 14th, the cavalry was in fact slithering and sliding about on the churned up, shell-pitted land around the original front lines a mile or so to the rear.

At about 7 p.m., however, the cavalry went into action on the open slope leading up towards High Wood. This became one of the most famous, if one of the most pointless, actions of the whole war. At long last the cavalry were seen in action. Was there to be a war of movement again? For months afterwards men spoke of the Indian cavalry at High Wood as if to reassure themselves that there was still some glory left to war.

High Wood had been almost untouched by shell-fire. A machine-gun opened on the cavalry as they cleared the corn before the wood. Two squadrons each of the 20th Deccan Horse, and the 7th Dragoon Guards, continued to the edge of the wood, where they also came under shell-fire and sniping. Several German outposts lying in the corn were lanced to death before they had time to flee.

Supporting infantry found the sight before their eyes difficult to believe. Fields of corn in harvest, to a back-cloth of a luxuriant green wood, were not common sights on the Western Front. But to see the cavalry in action, their bugles sounding and pennants fluttering in the evening breeze, and the last rays of the sun before it set glittering on the troopers' lances, was a wonderful sight indeed. If those famous cavalrymen Generals Haig and Gough could have seen it, it would no doubt have done their hearts good.

All who took part in it spoke with exultation of getting away from the pocked battlefield to this scene reminiscent of another kind of war. Many of the supporting infantry cheered with excitement. The German commander here, Sixt von Armin, wrote: 'The frontal attacks over open ground against a portion of our unshaken infantry, carried out by several English cavalry regiments, which had to retire with heavy losses, give some indication of the tactical knowledge of the Higher Command.'

Rawlinson's vision of the part the cavalry would play in the assault of 14 July was a colourful but impossible pipe-dream. The result of the dawn attack of the 14th was that a good deal of the second German line was taken, including most of the ruins of Longueval and the Bazentins. At Delville wood, however, there had been fierce fighting, giving some indication that it might be even more difficult to capture the whole of the German second position than it had been to take the first. The line was double throughout; there was a concrete fort nearly every fifty yards, and the second line of this second system was probably even stronger than the first.

On Saturday the 15th the newly arrived South African divisions were ordered to take Delville Wood 'at all costs'. They took about half the wood after a few hours' fighting, but from then on the Germans rained a barrage of shells down on them that never ceased. Dense columns of smoke rose from the shattered mess. A survivor said the ground was 'strewn every yard with the rags of human bodies'. Said another: 'Nothing could live outside the dug-outs.' Most of the South Africans in the northern part of the wood were killed. Heavy rain increased their misery.

Although British troops in Delville Wood were relieved, some South Africans were there for as long as five days, somehow clinging on to life through the murderous barrage, and some of them even returned. Even the company of engineers attached to them was relieved – but not the South Africans. Someone seemed to have forgotten about them, or perhaps it was true, as many of them thought, that Empire troops always got the dirty jobs, because the British commanders would not have to answer to Empire politicians for their conduct.

This is not to say that British troops which were pumped through the supply line to the wood had any better fortunes. The 2nd Suffolks were one of several battalions almost annihilated when they attacked on the 20th. They were meant to be joined by the 10th Royal Welch Fusiliers who had been misled by a guide in the tangled mess of the wood. When zero hour arrived the Suffolks went on alone, their right flank entirely exposed. The Fusiliers turned up ten minutes later, consequently coming under British machine-gun fire, to which they lost practically all their officers.

That night, the 20th, the remnants of the South African Brigade were relieved from Delville Wood. They had been in action earlier in the year against the Senussi in Egypt, but they had never before experienced anything like this. In Delville Wood ('Devil's Wood') their life had been hell on earth. Their machine-guns were eventually all knocked out, so when the Germans counter-attacked they had to stand up in the trenches and fire with rifles (an unusual procedure on the Somme). When they were taken prisoners many of them were shot.

Private J. A. Lawson, of the 3rd South African Infantry, wrote a booklet on his experiences called *Memories of Delville Wood*.

A drizzling rain was falling in an atmosphere unstirred by a breath of wind. Smoke and gases clung to and polluted the air, making a canopy impervious to light. What a contrast was this Tuesday morning to the previous Saturday, when we first entered what was then a beautiful sylvan scene, but now everywhere a dreary waste. Midday came and with it a midday meal eaten under this filthy pall. During the whole of this day No Man's Land was enveloped in semi-darkness, making it impossible to see anything but blurred outlines.

After barrage and infantry attacks for four days, he wrote:

Once more they had failed. The top of our trench told more plainly than words how near they were to not failing. Exhaustion did what shell-fire and counter-attacks had failed to do, and we collapsed in our trench, spent in body and at last worn out in spirit. The task we had been set was too great for us. What happened during the next two hours or so I do not know. Numbed in all my senses, I gazed vacantly into space, feeling as if the whole thing had been a ghastly nightmare, out of which I was now only waiting complete deliverance.

After a near-hit by a shell, Lawson was wakened from his coma. He staggered down the trench.

Only six remained alive in the trench. I aroused one of the sleepers and told him that I had been badly hit and was going to try and walk out. He faced me for a moment and asked me what he was going to do. I said there was nothing to do but carry on, as the orders of Saturday morning had not been countermanded. His brave 'Right O!' were the last words I heard there.

Delville Wood is now laid out as a memorial to the South Africans.

Robert Graves, luckily for future generations, but not so luckily for himself as he was seriously wounded, was by now up in the line. His battalion of Welshmen relieved one of Tyneside Irish. He asked one of their officers where the Germans were. 'He said he didn't know, but pointed vaguely towards Martinpuich, a mile to our front. Then I asked him who held our left flank, and how far off they were. He didn't know.'

Their Irish guide, detailed to bring them to the position, 'was hysterical and had forgotten the way'. During a bombardment Graves had the strange experience of a mouse slipping past his collar and down his neck for fear of the shells.

The whisper went round: 'Get your rifles ready. Here comes Fritz!' I lay flat on my face to see better, and some seventy yards away in the moonlight, made out massed figures...The men seemed to be under no proper command: we wondered why. There had been a number of German surrenders recently at night, and this might be one on a big scale. Deciding to give the enemy a chance, [we] sent up a flare and fired a Lewis gun over their heads. The tall officer who came running towards us, his hands lifted in surrender, seemed surprised to find that we were not Germans. He claimed that he belonged to the Public Schools' Battalion in our own brigade. [His] patrol consisted of fifty men, wandering about aimlessly between the lines, their rifles slung, and, it seemed, without the faintest idea where they were, or what information they were supposed to secure.

Graves's company got an order from brigade to build two strong-points at a certain map reference. When he and the company commander looked at the map, they burst into laughter. The points selected were behind the enemy lines.

During an attack on High Wood, Graves's battalion received a message from division.

Division could always be trusted to send a warning about verdigris on vermoral-sprayers, or the keeping of pets in trenches, or being polite to our allies, or some other triviality, exactly when an attack was in progress. This time orders came for a private in 'C' Company to report immediately under escort of a lance-corporal, to the assistant provost-marshal back at Albert, where a court martial had been convened. A sergeant of the company must also report as a witness in the case.

After the attack Graves was reported dead on his twenty-first birthday. Only eighty men were left in his battalion.

High Wood was not entirely in British hands until mid-September, and Delville Wood not until the end of August. Throughout the remainder of July and August, and the first half of September, bitter fighting continued around the woods; a few yards would be won somewhere one day, a few yards lost somewhere else on the next.

During the three weeks that the Somme Battle had been raging so far, Joffre continually pressed Haig to renew the offensive on the whole front, instead of just concentrating on the part where gains had been made on 1 July. Haig did not feel able to do this, but in order to more fully engage Gough's

Army, now known as the Reserve or Fifth Army, he ordered it immediately to take the village of Pozières – just south of the Thiepval salient (which remained as impregnable as ever).

The unit assigned to this task was the Anzac Corps, which had come from forty-five miles farther up the line. Pozières, or the ruins of it, stood on a small hillock. It was at once a difficult place to attack, and a difficult one to hold, being a perfect target for concentrated artillery fire.

Only one division of the corps had actually arrived, and in his anxiety to carry out Haig's order, Gough decided to throw it in, despite the fact that its officers had had no time to acquaint themselves with the situation. When the Division's commander first reached Gough's H.Q. on the 18th, Gough greeted him thus: 'I want you to go into the line and attack Pozières tomorrow night!'

This struck the Australian as a hasty way of going about the attack of a place which had resisted planned assaults before. Gough was persuaded to delay it, and it eventually took place on Saturday, 23 July, and Pozières was successfully captured after considerable loss. Haig asked that the Australians should push on into the side of the Thiepval salient and make it untenable. The *Australian Official History* described the process that followed as: 'that of applying a battering ram ten or fifteen times against the same part of the enemy's battlefront with the intention of penetrating for a mile, or possibly two, into the midst of his organized defences.'

Nineteen attacks were launched by the Australians during this phase. And because neither Haig nor Gough insisted on other Corps launching their attacks at the same time during this so-called 'nibbling' period, the Germans were able to concentrate enormous artillery fire on one point – often on the Australians around Pozières. The bombardment here was even worse than that suffered by the South Africans at Delville Wood. For seven weeks the three Australian divisions endured this battering, one after the other taking over the line from the remainder of the others.

Ragged men lived in holes in the shaking ground, like moles. Life became one long, seemingly hopeless prayer for survival. Night and day the shells burst on the top of the hillock of Pozières. The fumes made a kind of perpetual fog. The ruins of the village, the remains of the orchards around it, bricks, bones, equipment, all were ground up into a soggy grey substance which from a distance could be seen smoking like a dying bonfire. A survivor recorded: 'Nothing but a churned mass of debris with bricks, stones and girders, and bodies pounded to nothing. There are not even tree trunks left, not a leaf, not a twig, all is buried, and churned up again, and buried again.'

No one in the rear, neither the Australian commanders, nor Haig, nor Gough, had any idea as to what the battle was like. They were several miles behind the line. Pozières was the name of a village on a map.

To get to the Australian lines at all was an achievement. Their position was such that they were under fire from all four directions, including the rear (from Thiepval). There was only one way to get to the line, except in individual groups of two or three (which could sometimes hope to get across the feature-less terrain unnoticed). This way led, at two points at least, across crests in full view of the Germans, who remorselessly barraged these points at any sign of movement. Yet food, water, ammunition and stores, all had to be hauled to the place that was once Pozières.

Practically wiped out, the remnants of the Australian divis-ions clung on; crouching in hastily dug holes as the screaming shells howled overhead or crashed into the smoking, churned-up substance that had once been a village. According to the official Australian historian the powdered debris was six feet deep; a sandbag-full of this muck is now in the Australian War Memorial at Canberra. It was no longer possible for anyone to say exactly where they were on the map. On one occasion the heavy artillery were about to bombard a trench when they were told by the staff of the 3rd Battalion that their own men were in it. The brigade staff, on the other hand, said that these men must be two hundred yards to the rear of the trench. The divisional staff worked out that they were in a third position. The twenty-four-year-old battalion commander, Lieutenant-Colonel O. Howell-Price, meanwhile found and stood on the only identifiable object in the vicinity, a powdery depression. He realized that this had once been a road cutting. From this he hurriedly worked out his position; the battalion staff had been right. But, as in a nightmare, his message to the rear was too late. He and his men were remorselessly shelled.

The following story gives some idea of the plain ignorance of those behind the line. During a particularly heavy bombard-ment an almost naked, exhausted Australian arrived on the hill with a message, having miraculously survived the barrage. He was an officer's servant, and the message he carried was from the division vet. It read: 'Sir, I have the honour to report that your old mare is suffering from an attack of the strangles.' The message was acknowledged, but it is not recorded in what terms.

Keeping trenches in some kind of shape under such conditions became a major task. One pioneer battalion lost two hundred and thirty men keeping open one section of one trench. Another lost eighty-five in a single night. It was difficult for the artillery exactly to locate the Australian lines, and they continually came under their own fire.

After an attack by the Australians on 28 July, which failed, Haig wrote in his diary:

> Impressed on Gough and his G.S.O. that they must supervise more closely the plans of the Anzac Corps. Some of their divisional generals are so ignorant and (like many Colonials) so conceited, that they cannot be trusted to work out unaided the plans of attack.

Haig was well known for bullying commanders to hasten their attacks, and for then being infuriated by their failure at what he called 'lack of preparation'.

Haig told Birdwood, commanding the Anzac Corps, that because he had achieved some success at Gallipoli he should not imagine that slap-dash methods would suffice against the Germans. He is reported to have said (by C. E. W. Bean in *Two Men I Knew*): 'You're not fighting Bashi-Bazouks now – this is serious, scientific war.'

On the following day these same 'Colonial' soldiers did a little better, but at one point they rushed over their objective unknowingly, this shell-shattered object being completely unrecognizable, and suffered heavily from their own barrage.

After setbacks and lack of progress all down the line, Haig now decided at last to stop launching any further attacks on a large scale until supplies, particularly artillery ammunition, had been built up again to a level where one more great push would finally break the enemy. He imagined this next great effort would take place about mid-September. Meantime, various parts of the line were to be straightened out, and the Germans worn down by continual fighting.

For the time being Haig had completely capitulated to Joffre's idea of a battle of attrition along the whole Somme front. The trouble was that neither of the Generals seemed to realize that the device of 'wearing down' merely succeeded in inflicting more casualties on themselves than it did on the enemy.

The battle of attrition was continued by the Fourth and Fifth Armies until 15 September, when the next large attack occurred. Fighting continued at Guillemont, Longueval, and Delville Wood, at High Wood, at Pozières, and the Thiepval salient, and at Mouquet Farm. Each has its stories of blunder, of heroism, of tragedy, and of bloodily won success. From day to day the battle went on, one day much like another.

The King visited the front, or quite near to it, and Haig enjoyed himself entertaining him.

I received him in the garden with my mounted Escort (twenty-nine of the 17th Lancers) and about fifty of the Artists Rifles. The King then came into my writing-room, and I explained the situation to him. He then spoke a great deal about a paper which Winston Churchill had written and given to the Cabinet, criticizing the operations in France, and arriving at the conclusion that nothing had been achieved. The King also said that much harm was being done at home by the Generals who had been sent back as useless from France. They formed a regular Cabal and abused everything that was done by the British H.Q. on the Western Front.

On 12 August they had lunch at Haig's Château de Valvion at Beauquesne. President Poincaré was present; he urged the King to encourage Haig to attack ceaselessly along the entire Somme frontage.

We had 15 at lunch, and by the King's desire, only water of various kinds was served [Lloyd George had persuaded George V to give up drink for the war, as an example to the factory workers]. Many of us will long remember General Joffre's abhorrence, or annoyance, when Shaddock (my butler) handed him a jug of lemonade and a bottle of ginger beer, and asked him which he preferred.

Haig's policy produced a strange way of life, if it could be called that, at the front. Those who shared the horrors of the front have, on the whole, been surprisingly reticent about it, considering that nearly a whole generation fought there. Afterwards, some only wished to forget; others, like Osbert Sitwell (in *Laughter in the Next Room*) found that when they came to write about it their memories refused to recall the horror. It has become a kind of half-secret, shared by those who were there, but presumed to be incommunicable to those who were not. Haig himself, for instance, probably never had a true idea of what life in a forward trench was like till the day he died.

To try to give some impression of this bare-existence, however, a few people put their observations down on paper, and later some of these writings found their way into print. In the case of the vivid descriptions of Lieutenant M. St. Helier Evans this did not happen until 1952. On 27 July, in a letter home, he wrote:

I write from a so-called shelter in this newly dug line. My right flank is in the air so to speak, it does not even peter out, it ends abruptly a few yards from a ruined tower, or was it a windmill more likely. A few yards ahead hanging in the wire like a collapsed scarecrow is the remains of a once human; it is now black as a Negro, stiff and brittle. Every time a certain gun fires this body jerks like a marionette; it is worrying the men, we must get it buried after dark.

On Monday 24th we had a nerve racking time, an overdose of concentrated hate lasting three solid hours. Every shell they had seemed to be hurled at this trench; they were bent on destruction. We experienced the torments of hell; this is perhaps hell itself purging us if we deserve it for the hereafter. During this excruciating avalanche, we crouched or lay flat on the floor of our ditch, shrapnel burst above our heads, and rattled on our helmets, we got our faces and clothes covered with powder, earth and fine dust churned up. Missiles of all calibres fell on all sides.

Would any of us be allowed to live, to love, to marry and beget children, to taste the pleasures of all that a full life promised? But why grumble, we were paid to be here at five shillings a day and the men rich on a shilling.

A Very light went up and we went down, flopped down on our hands and found them touching cold jelly-like swollen faces; we slithered and rocked and lost balance on wobbling bloated bellies. It was a Jerry graveyard or would have been had they been properly buried. The stench was indescribable.

We had our clothes on for ten days, without taking them off I mean, and never a wash or shave.

On 3 September he wrote:

We hear on good authority how a man was shot for cowardice; the volley failed to kill, the officer in charge of the firing squad lost his nerve and instead of emptying his revolver into the writhing body, turned to the A.P.M. and said: 'Do your own bloody work, I cannot.' We understand the sequel was that he was arrested.

Everyone who had been on the Somme for a week was a cynic. There was no trace of the jolly 'Tommy' of legend. Everyone was miserable and shocked.

Because of the enormous death roll, extraordinary promotions and mix-ups had taken place. At least one Colonel with a substantive rank of Lieutenant was walking around with an eye-patch and a black-gloved hand. Many of the best and most experienced men were casualties. 'The loss of their enterprise and resource,' says the *Official History,* 'was severely felt.' The War Office had deliberately insisted that reinforcements and returning wounded should be posted to regiments other than their own. This lessened regimental spirit and caused deep resentment.

Because of the barrages, the army dragged behind it an ever-lengthening trail of ruin and soggy land as it slowly pushed forward, while the Germans retired to clean land and good roads.

Edmund Blunden was fighting during this autumn period at the famous 'Jacob's Ladder' trench and later near Auchonvilliers ('Ocean Villas'). He records in *Undertones of War* how his R.S.M. was told to make dummy men of straw in order to draw enemy fire while another hopeless attack was made on the great Thiepval stronghold. Of course, there was no straw. Straw was about the last thing to be found lying around at the front. The bewildered but resourceful R.S.M., however, somehow managed to manufacture 190 dummies.

Blunden records the rumours continually going down the line; of a spy in a soft cap and mac (General Bridges, commanding the 19th Division which had six thousand five hundred casualties in July alone, removed the distinctive red band from his cap because of the danger of being shot by these legendary spies); of the rumour that no winter campaign might be necessary.

L. W. Griffith wrote of the area behind the line:

Transport was crawling about in the distance, small groups of men were moving, dark against the white gashes in the chalk. Scattered equipment lying about under foot, tangles of wire, small dumps of forgotten stores, all left behind in the advance. Other things were left behind, part of the purchase of this downland, grim disfigured corpses rotting in the sun, so horrible in their discolour that it called for an act of faith to believe that these were once men, young men, sent to this degradation by their fellow men.

Paragraph 219 of the pre-war *Land Warfare* stated: 'Before the dead are buried they must be carefully examined to see that life is extinct.'

Mark Plowman, in his *A Subaltern on the Somme* (by 'Mark VII'), also gives a description of the old battlefield, over which all supplies had to be dragged:

The country here is stricken waste, the trees that formed an avenue to the road are now torn and broken stumps, some still holding unexploded shells in their shattered trunks, others looped about with useless telegraph wire. The earth on both sides of the road is churned up into a crumbling mass, and so tossed and scarred is the ground that the actual line of the front trenches is hardly distinguishable ... a wilderness without verdure or growth of any kind.

Lying around were the debris of war; dead horses, wire, bombs, bully-beef tins, rags, broken rifles, rounds of ammunition, mess-tins, bits of leather and webbing, British and German battered steel helmets, iron stakes, skulls white and clean. Here and there were improvised graves – an inverted bottle with a piece of paper in it, a stick with a forage cap, a rough wooden cross.

Digging trenches in this area was a horrible task as described by 'Mark VII'.

Hill returned from it last night physically sick. There are men buried here four or five feet deep. Their bodies often lying as they fell, with the limbs stretched transversely above the gap, must be imagined, for they will not be described.

Men at the front were, in fact, living among the dead. Corpses were lying around everywhere. Young boys just out of school became thoroughly hardened to death.

Sometimes [wrote A. D. Gristwood in *The Somme*], the

Germans had buried the dead in the floor of the trench, where, baking in the sun, the earth had cracked into star-shaped fissures. A foot treading unwarily here sank down-wards, disturbing hundreds of white maggots. In one place a hand with blue and swollen fingers projected helplessly from the ground. Close to the trench a man stood nearly upright, buried to the waist, his arms fast bound to his sides, his glassy eyes wide open to the sky, his face stained livid yellow from the fumes of an explosion. Who he was no one knew; doubtless his dear ones were still writing to him in hope and trust for his welfare; doubtless they had prayed that night for his safety. And all the time he stood there, glaring upwards as though mutely appealing from Earth to Heaven.

Wrote Mark Plowman:

The air is tainted with the sickly-sweet odour of decaying bodies. At certain corners this odour, intensified by the heat, becomes a stench so foul the bay cannot be occupied. Just now I tripped over a lump in the floor of the trench. It was necessary to get a shovel and quickly cover the spot.

People at home are horrified by the thought of lice, but they seem a very minor ill here. No one who sees much of the front line is altogether free from them. They are a curse when the body becomes heated.

About the only pleasure Plowman could find were the stars in the sky: 'What joy it is to know that you in England and I out here at least can look upon the same beauty in the sky.' During a bombardment, 'at moments there is real silence. To our tired ears this absence of sound is positive and acute pleas-ure; we drink it like wine, loath to break it even with conversa-tion.'

Crouching in 'funk holes' (niches cut beneath the parapet), men somehow survived. They ate bully-beef and bread. They were supplied with water in petrol tins, which not surprisingly tasted of petrol. There is no doubt that some men would have committed suicide if the rum ration had been withdrawn. Many officers were alcoholics, seeing the whole thing through a nightmarish haze.

To try to keep up their spirits, men sang and whistled. Nos-talgic songs, or the most sentimental ones, were the only songs popular at the front: 'I Want to Go Home', 'The Long Trail',

'Tennessee'. Songs about mother were particularly well liked. 'Roses round the door, make me love mother more.'

At this time there was much use of tear shells, that made little noise, but which caused the eyes to water and destroyed uncovered food. It was morale-sapping, not least because it made smoking difficult.

Before a 'stunt', the whole day's rations were distributed. Straps and buckles were adjusted over greatcoats; rifles, gas-masks, groundsheets slung, last letters written once more. And wearily the infantry would go over the top when ordered to do so, wondering if they could possibly get through yet another 'show' unscathed. As the weeks went on, sheer nervous exhaustion overcame many, causing hundreds of needless deaths. The regimental history of the Royal Ulster Rifles speaks of men, after days of fighting, collapsing on the battlefield and lying down fast asleep with grenades falling all around them.

Life at the front was, as always, incomprehensible to those at home. During the famous battles for the woods the public had visions of men crawling, Red Indian style, through the undergrowth, using skill and initiative in a romantic war.

Meanwhile, Douglas Haig motored about behind the line, from H.Q. to H.Q., from lunch to lunch. After yet another unsuccessful attack on Thiepval, which had by now accounted for many thousands of British soldiers, he wrote in his diary:

The units of that Division did not really attack, and some men did not follow their officers. I had occasion a fortnight ago to call the attention of the Army and Corps Commanders (Gough and Jacob) to the lack of smartness, and slackness of one of its Battalions in the matter of saluting when I was motoring through the village where it was billeted. I expressed my opinion that such men were too sleepy to fight well.

And so the massacre went on, and the days grew shorter and colder.

CHAPTER SIXTEEN

'TANKS'

Now it was time for a strange, clanking, clumsy machine to make its awkward appearance on the drab, dismal battlefields of the Somme, much to the astonishment of all those who saw it – and the fury of those who had invented it.

There was nothing surprising about the invention of the tank. It was the obvious logical adaptation of the automobile to warfare – especially trench warfare. Several inventors had suggested the idea in pre-war days, in England, Austria, and Germany. H. G. Wells, needless to say, had thought of it. Caterpillar tractors were being used as early as 1908 by the Army for haulage purposes, and E. D. Swinton brought the matter up in 1914. He was a Major in the Engineers and his suggestion met with a frosty reception from the military authorities. Winston Churchill, First Lord of the Admiralty, however, was also investigating along the same lines, and when his suggestion was turned down, he, unlike Swinton, had both the financial means and the authority to go on alone.

His memo to Mr. Asquith on 5 January 1915 was an historic one. It contained the following points among many others:

It is extraordinary that the Army in the Field and the War Office should have allowed nearly three months of trench warfare to progress without addressing their minds to its special problems. It would be quite easy in a short time to fit up a number of steam tractors with small armoured shells, in which men and machine-guns could be placed, which would be bullet-proof. The caterpillar system would enable trenches to be crossed quite easily, and the weight of the machine would destroy all wire entanglements.

Churchill's memorandum had no effect and the suggestion was 'interred in the archives of the War Office'. Undeterred, Churchill provided, on his own responsibility, money from Admiralty funds for further experiments (about seventy thousand pounds). He did not inform the Treasury or the War Office. He admits it was a serious decision to spend this large sum of money on a project so speculative, about the merits of which no high expert military or naval authority had been convinced. Had the tanks proved wholly abortive, I could have offered no effective defence to the charge that I had wasted public money.

He ordered eighteen tanks.

But Churchill left the Admiralty in May 1915, after Gallipoli, and the project was almost scrapped because of 'the general disfavour in which my affairs were at this time involved'. He managed to persuade his successor, Arthur Balfour, to continue with the construction of one machine. This tank was displayed at Hatfield Park in February 1916. It was the exact model of the ones which fought at the Somme (both the 'males', with 6-pounder guns, and the 'females', with machine-guns only).

Lloyd George, Minister of Munitions, at a previous demonstration, was understandably 'surprised to find that these experiments were being conducted by naval men'.

Lloyd George was present at the Hatfield Park demonstration as well, which was a great success.

I can recall the feeling of delighted amazement with which I saw for the first time the ungainly monster, bearing the inscription 'H.M.S. *Centipede*' on its breast, plough through thick entanglements, wallow through deep mud, and heave its huge bulk over parapets and various trenches. At last, I thought, we have the answer to the German machine-guns and wire. Mr. Balfour's delight was as great as my own, and it was only with difficulty that some of us persuaded him to disembark from H.M. Landship whilst she crossed the last test, a trench several feet wide.

All this had been done with the active hostility of those military leaders who knew about it, and the ignorance of the army's exact requirements was a severe handicap in the construction of the tank (so called as inquisitive people seeing the secret machine travelling by train could be fobbed off with the answer 'It's a tank'). A deputation sent to France for this purpose were 'obliged to return' without any information whatever.

But now the generals changed their tune. After the Hatfield Park demonstration, they promptly ordered a hundred 'tanks'. Swinton was put in charge of raising and commanding the new unit which was to man them. Haig suddenly became enthusiastic. He wanted them as soon as possible, and on 26 August he was shown a demonstration of the tanks in France.

In defence of the generals concerned in the blood-baths of the Western Front it is often stated that there was nothing else any commander could have done. There was stalemate, and no possibility of strategy apart from the process of attrition, or bloody attempts at battering a way through with enormous numbers of men. Winston Churchill, of course, had never been satisfied that this was so, and he had now produced the very thing that could be an effective answer to the stalemate.

All those concerned with the introduction and production of the tanks were convinced of one thing: the first time they were to be used, they must be in the largest numbers possible. Only in this way could their quality of surprise, which they were about to reintroduce to warfare, be fully utilized. There was a fear that the Army would waste this vital asset by using them here and there in small numbers as they became available. Swinton, Churchill, and Lloyd George saw that it was their first use that mattered. Soon it would be winter, when they would be useless in the mud, and the Germans forewarned would be able to construct pits and devise other means to combat the new weapon. Ceaselessly they warned Haig and his staff on this point, and on 29 July the Commander-in-Chief replied that he was 'fully alive to the disadvantages of using the tanks before the full number on order was available'.

Meantime, Haig had been planning his great attack which was to push forward the British line still farther on the Somme, after constant cajoling and bullying by Joffre. In a secret report to London, he stressed that the battle was necessary in order to give 'the enemy no rest and no respite from anxiety'. He was also, of course, committing his forces to the same punishment. By this time the crisis at Verdun had passed long ago, and the fact that this was the later reason for the battle being waged at all, and before Haig was even ready for it, seemed to have been forgotten. Early on in his life, Haig had shown himself a stubborn man. Now, as a general, one of his major failings was that once he had started a battle he was not prepared to call it off until it was obvious to all that it was a great victory (a contingency that seldom, if ever, occurred), despite the losses of thousands of his best troops.

But Douglas Haig now proceeded to show another major failing; irresponsibility. In the circumstances, his action now was quite inexcusable. He knew there were rumours about his leadership at home. He knew it was important that the new phase of the Somme offensive was a success. He ordered that all tanks completed should be sent to France immediately, as he intended to use them shortly. Ignoring all the expert and logical advice, to which he had previously agreed, he was now about to throw away the one thing that, if properly used, could turn the whole course of the war in a few hours.

It had been pointed out to Haig that the crews of the tanks were not yet fully trained; that no practice had been carried out with infantry, the commanders of which had not the faintest idea of how to co-operate with the machines; that according to the engineers who manufactured them the existing ones were practically worn out after the many miles covered in demonstration and trials; that they were partly obsolescent, having been designed in accordance with the trenches of 1915; above all, that as many as five hundred tanks might be available if he could wait until January.

The first six machines left for France on 15 August. Haig wrote to the C.I.G.S., Sir William Robertson, that he hoped for fifty tanks for the attack.

> Even if I do not get so many as I hope, I shall use what I have got, as I cannot wait any longer for them, and it would be folly not to use every means at my disposal in what is likely to be our crowning effort for this year.

This is in strange contrast to Haig's remark on 29 July and his agreement in February 1916, to a paper circulated by Swinton on the tactics to be employed in the use of the tank. This had stated:

> The chance of success of the new arm lies in its ability to effect a complete surprise, and therefore the machines should not be used in driblets; the fact of their existence should be kept secret until the whole are ready to be launched together.

Even the French, who had been let into the secret, pleaded that there should be no premature use of the machines. A Lieutenant-Colonel of the new unit also protested – so violently that he was promptly replaced.

Lloyd George told Churchill of Haig's decision. Churchill

was horrified and, although much out of favour there, he went to Number Ten, Downing Street, and begged Asquith to stop Haig before it was too late. Asquith, as was his habit, listened attentively, agreed with what was said, argued with Haig, and achieved absolutely nothing. Lloyd George also saw Asquith and 'begged him to intervene. He did not disagree . . . but referred me to the C.I.G.S. So the great secret was sold for the battred ruin of a little hamlet.'

Edwin Montagu, who had replaced Lloyd George (War Minister after Kitchener's death) at the Ministry of Munitions, also pleaded with Asquith. All these men were the kind that Haig called 'the grousers in London'. They were the wretched amateurs, so it seemed to him, who were constantly trying to stop him from winning the war.

CHAPTER SEVENTEEN

A VITAL ERROR

JUST before the attack commenced Lloyd George visited Haig, for the first time as War Minister. Here he had, it would seem, a perfect opportunity to inform Haig personally of his misgivings about the coming use of the tanks. But there is no record of him having do so. Unfortunately, no politician appears to have stood up to Haig in person during the war on the Western Front, although plenty of them said what they thought of his methods behind his back.

In a letter to his wife, Haig wrote:

Lloyd George has been with me during the past two days; so I have been able to notice the differences in the two men and to realize how much superior in many ways Mr. Asquith is to L.G. I have got on with the latter very well indeed, and he is anxious to help in every way he can. Most unpunctual (*except* when coming to meet me, I must confess). The P.M.'s visit was on business lines; L.G.'s has been a huge 'joy ride'! Breakfasts with Newspaper men, and posings for the Cinema Shows, pleased him more than anything else. No doubt with the ulterior object of catching votes. From what I have written you will gather that I have no great opinion of Lloyd George *as a man or leader*.

Haig was getting on with his preparations for the coming battle during Lloyd George's visit. Despite the advent of the tank, he and Rawlinson yet again provided for a large force of cavalry (five divisions) to be massed behind the front, ready to charge through the expected gap in the enemy's line. The instructions for the cavalry, after they had reached the German rear, were to 'interfere' with the railways, along which 'hostile reinforcements' might arrive, and to raid the various enemy H.Q.s which were seven or eight miles behind the front. Despite their apparent appreciation of the tank, both men at heart still felt that the war was to be won with lances and sabres.

Lloyd George noted:

I have driven through squadrons of cavalry clattering

133

proudly to the front. When I asked what they were for, Sir Douglas Haig explained that they were brought up as near the front line as possible, so as to be ready to charge through the gap which was to be made by the Guards in the coming attack. The cavalry were to exploit the anticipated success and finish the German rout.

Lloyd George comments on how the attack failed, and how Raymond Asquith, the brilliant son of the Prime Minister, one of the most promising men of his generation, was killed with many of his contemporaries. 'When I ventured to express my doubts as to whether cavalry could ever operate successfully on a front bristling for miles behind the enemy's line with barbed wire and machine-guns, both Generals fell on me.' Joffre pointed out that he himself intended a large cavalry charge next morning on his own front.

During a visit to Foch, Lloyd George asked the French General why the British, who gained no more ground than the French, had suffered such heavy casualties. But Foch was loyal to his fellow soldier, said he had no means of forming an opinion, and told Haig about it. Haig was incensed. 'Unless I had been told of this conversation personally by General Foch,' he wrote in his diary, 'I would not have believed that a British Minister could have been so ungentlemanly as to go to a foreigner and put such questions regarding his own subordinates.'

The massing of the force of cavalry severely complicated the problems of supply, but by 15 September all was ready, and the usual terrific bombardment, lasting three days, was almost complete, and had warned the enemy of the coming attack. Both the Armies, Rawlinson's and Gough's, were to take part in the assault, and of the forty-nine tanks available forty-two were allotted to the former and the remainder to Gough. Most of them had only arrived at the front directly in time to go into action. Their crews had hardly slept in over forty-eight hours. In spite of tapes and guides, many of the tanks did not manage to get over the old battlefield behind the starting point, with its muddy craters and churned-up ground. Some got stuck in shell holes, others fell through the tops of disused dug-outs. In the end, thirty-six arrived at their assembly places, of which less than a dozen played any effective part in the battle that ensued.

Their presence in the area had been suspected by the Germans, who knew of some kind of armoured vehicle that was expected to attack. This information had not infiltrated down to all ranks, however, and some panic was caused in certain units – but there was no widespread demoralization such as there certainly would have taken place if five hundred of the machines had been suddenly launched at the unsuspecting infantry. A few Germans took to their heels when they saw the things lumbering towards them. One horrified prisoner said in English that they were 'not war but bloody butchery'. Other Germans successfully bombed them.

Some of the tanks lost their direction, some were indiscriminately ordered to return by confused infantry officers, some cruised about aimlessly until they were hit. The fact was that their drivers and commanders (they held eight men) were not sufficiently trained in their control or in the useful part they could play in co-operation with infantry.

Meanwhile, the Germans were hurrying up reinforcements, the initiative was lost, and the advance faded out after out after a belt of about two thousand five hundred yards had been taken. It was clear by the afternoon that the great autumn offensive had failed and that objectives would not be reached.

Four tanks actually reached the village of Flers, and one clattered through the battered main street followed by cheering troops and returned safely. Most of the remainder were hit and caught fire, or were ditched.

The French did not co-operate in the battle, and continued to delay entering into the heavy fighting which followed. They took little part until the 25th, when another attack was launched. It was the anniversary of the British reverse at Loos, and Charteris, Haig's intelligence chief, wrote in his diary ' . . . a great difference between this year and last'. He was not attempting irony. On 27 September the Thiepval spur was at last taken, having held out since 1 July. A battalion of the Bedfordshires were the ones who finally took possession. The land surrounding this stronghold was carpeted with British corpses from the numerous previous attacks which had failed.

The remainder of the tanks were given over to Gough, and they were used for the rest of the Somme Battle singly or in small groups, their effectiveness being negligible. Haig ordered a thousand more, but this order was mysteriously cancelled by the War Office, which still had no faith in the machines (when he discovered it, Lloyd George countermanded this decision).

During the September offensive the villages of Courcelette (by the Canadians), Martinpuich (by the Scots), Flers and Guinchy were captured – as well as the strongpoints of Mouquet Farm, Schwaben Redoubt and, at last, High Wood.

Tanks were used in a haphazard way for the rest of the war, many being ordered to uselessly advance into the quagmire around Passchendaele in 1917, where they floundered and provided simple targets for German gunners. Says Churchill:

It took the High Command nearly two whole years to learn to use tanks in the manner and conditions for which they were originally conceived. During the interval every conceivable error was committed, which lack of comprehension could suggest. This priceless conception containing, if used in its integrity and on a sufficient scale, the certainty of a great and brilliant victory, was revealed to the Germans for the mere petty purpose of taking a few ruined villages.

In London, a film was to be seen at the Scala, showing scenes of cheery columns of men marching into action. It was about the Battle of the Somme, and it proved to be one of the most popular films yet made. It was the talking point of society, and it was necessary for everyone to go to see it. It did not, by any means, convey the horror of the autumn battle-front.

Thirteen airships attacked London on 2 September, and everyone was much excited, and felt that they too were really in the war now. The leaves had fallen in the London squares, and the glow from cosy fireplaces lit the darkening windows of houses in Bloomsbury and Belgravia. Wounded were coming back in such streams that many had to be diverted from Charing Cross and taken right round London to Paddington. The casualties of 1 July and subsequent attacks were recovering, or dying, in the crowded, improvised hospital wards. One of the convalescent, wounded on 1 July, wrote:

People made a fuss of the wounded, though we who were not badly hurt knew we were lucky. Life became very sweet – except for thoughts of friends still at the front.

Letters came from the boys. Then there were fewer letters. The battalion was in attack after attack. How many were left of those who had joined in the opening weeks of the war? Anyway, I would be going out again, and it was up to me to make the best of these days. That was the winter when water-bottles at the front became ice-bottles.

The C.I.G.S. busied himself by writing worried little notes to 'Aig:

> The powers that be are beginning to get a little uneasy in regard to the situation. The casualties are mounting up, and Ministers are wondering whether we are likely to get a proper return for them. I do my best to keep the general situation to the front and to explain what may be the effect of our efforts, and to ask what alternative could be adopted. I also try to make them think in German terms of the present situation. But they will persist in asking me whether I think a loss of, say, 300,000 men will lead to really great results, because if not we ought to be content with something less than what we are now doing and they constantly inquire why we are fighting and the French not. In general what is bothering them is the probability that we may soon have to face a bill of between 200,000 and 300,000 casualties with no very great gains additional to the present. It is thought that the primary objective– the relief of Verdun – has to some extent been achieved.

While Robertson pondered in the War Office on the fate that had placed him so uncomfortably between the frightening Scotsman and the nagging politicians he couldn't understand, the majority of the rest of the citizens of London were taking life more easily. The months of October and November saw one of the most brilliant and gay theatrical seasons on the London stage for many years. There was a Cochrane review at the Ambassadors, Gerald du Maurier at Wyndhams, *Hobson's Choice* at the Apollo, *Daddy Long Legs* at the Duke of York's, and A. E. Matthews in *Peg o' My Heart* at the Globe. Beecham was conducting a Grand Opera Season, and Sir Henry Wood was at the Queen's Hall. For those with lighter tastes, who wanted a little music-hall, something racy and something sentimental, there was a feast from which to choose in the evening papers. Little Tich was at the Hippodrome, and Grock and many other great names were appearing for the boys on leave. On 17 November, a matinée was held, in which nearly all the stars of the day appeared, at the London Opera House in Kingsway. The proceeds were to provide for 'Christmas puddings for soldiers at the front'. The Bing Boys were still playing to full houses at the Alhambra.

By now, news of the Somme Battle was off the main news pages of the papers. Despatches from the front were relegated to minor positions on secondary pages. The main news was of fighting in Romania, which had caught the public's fancy. A controversy was raging between the Reichstag and Westminster, *via* Amsterdam, as to the origin of the war. The Automobile Show opened at the Royal Agricultural Hall.

Fathers and brothers might be away, but children still had to go to school. Rupert Croft-Cooke recalls in *The Altar in the Loft* what it was like to be thirteen years old in 'that glorious summer'.

> The war remained remote. The terrible battle of the Somme in which there was such carnage that its deathroll even now, after Stalingrad and Hiroshima, looks like a madman's row of ciphers, was scarcely a name to me or to any other boy of my age.

A 'Lady Expert' was in attendance at Harvey Nichols each day 'to assist Mistresses requiring domestic servants'. Argentine Railways were rising, rubber was steady, and Royal Dutch oils were doing nicely. There was stormy weather, with bad fogs, and there were large advertisements for raincoats in the papers and magazines. Lady Baden-Powell attended a rally of Girl Guides on Barnes Common. Lloyd George went to Westminster Abbey to hear the *Elijah*: 'One of the finest performances I have ever listened to.'

Things were not as they had been once, but it was generally agreed that they could have been a lot worse.

After a short spell of leave in London, St. Helier Evans wrote in his diary:

> All time seems measured from 1 July. And the slaughter has been going on ever since. It is all very well for London to remain gay, but it seemed to me on leave that there was no realization of what we undergo out here.

CHAPTER EIGHTEEN

MUD

'The spectacle of attrition is distressing'
CAPT. CYRIL FALLS, *The Times*, 1958

DURING October and November desultory fighting continued on the Somme, although conditions got worse and worse, and the mud which had started becoming a serious problem in September became catastrophic. Minor attacks were launched against various villages and strong-points on the German line, all of which involved the customary despatch of infantry into the range of machine-gun fire and resulted in heavy casualties. Fighting and artillery fire took place every day without respite down the whole line. The records of a hundred years showed that October was the worst month of the year in the Somme valley (Charteris had carefully worked this out).

The battlefield turned into a vast sea of mud, churned up by machines, struggling animals and men, and shell-fire. But the battle continued, directed by men who never saw the field. Men wallowed and floundered in slime. Their food and ammunition disappeared on the choked roadways behind them. Their trenches were obliterated. The landscape was a wilderness of mire – known to the troops as 'porridge'.

These miserable weeks are officially known as the Battle of the Transloy Ridges 1-20 October, and the Battle of the Ancre Heights (10 October-11 November). The second was entirely the concern of Gough's Fifth Army, which began to take over more and more of the offensive, Rawlinson's Fourth Army being thoroughly exhausted, and because Joffre was now crying more than ever for greater efforts in the northern part of the line which had remained static since 1 July. Divisions there had lost thousands of men and never advanced so much as one inch. Most of the fighting took place around Le Sars and the Ancre Valley, and once more Canadians and Australians were heavily involved. Whenever the French co-operated, they almost invariably attacked later than the British (this, of course, provided them the element of surprise). Such were the conditions, however, that progress was negligible, despite the use of gas which lingered about above the wilderness in a yellow mist, giving a total impression as close to that of Hell as most men could conceive.

Mud, which was of a glutinous variety owing to the clay, balled on the soles of boots to the size of a football, making every step a vile torture. Men died from the effort of carrying messages; many died from slow drowning in mud; whole units disappeared; wounded were often suffocated in the mire before stretcher bearers could get to them. Because of the ceaseless shelling there was nothing that could be done to improve the situation. There was not a building or tree standing for miles. Nature's equation of grass and vegetation that counteracted the heavy rainfall had all been destroyed.

Mark Plowman wrote of the November trenches on the Somme:

> Corpses lie along the parapets, rotting in the wet: every now and then a booted foot appears jutting over the trench. The mud makes it all but impassable, and now sunk in up to the knees, I have the momentary terror of never being able to pull myself out. Such horror gives frenzied energy, and I tear my legs free and go on ... at arm's length from me a body has fallen face downward in the water ... while the trenches are in this condition we can neither get to the Germans nor them to us. Both sides are glued where they stand, so that Heaven alone knows what purpose we serve here, or whether we shall ever get out again. Like so many grotesque monuments, the men sit huddled under their groundsheets at their places beneath the parapet ... chits continue to come detailing the work expected of us, and [we] continue to reply that instructions are noted; but little or nothing is done, for the simple reason that the deity has not yet constructed men able to make or repair trenches when the earth at every step holds them immobile ... shovels are perfectly useless ... rain has been falling almost continuously for two days.

Much of the fighting took place round the Butte de Warlencourt, a chalk mound sixty feet high, which gave an excellent observation post to whichever side possesed it. This strange crater-pocked freak, imbedded itself in the minds of those who saw it in the winter of 1916 for ever. 'Charles Edmonds' (C. E. Carrington) wrote:

To go or come from the line was a nightmare adventure and, once there, one dared not move for fear of the enemy machine-guns on the Butte of Warlencourt,. That ghastly hill, never free from the smoke of bursting shells, became fabulous. It shone white in the night and seemed to leer at you lige an ogre in a fairy tale. It loomed up unexpectedly, peering into trenches where you thought yourself safe; it haunted your dreams. Twenty-four hours in the trenches before the Butte finished a man off.

Most of the little fighting that was done was hand to hand, and bayonets, rifles, and Lewis guns became clogged with mud from which it was impossible to protect them. As they carried out orders to attack the Butte, troops slipped and slithered in the mud and fell into water-logged shell holes. Some who were too exhausted to go farther, sank down and were left to perish. Others lost their boots, and even socks, in the ooze. One unit arrived at the German trenches without a boot or sock between them. One officer lost his trousers as well; Highlanders crossed No Man's Land without their kilts. These last facts are all recorded in the *Official History*; there are many witnesses to drownings in mud.

Many, the official Australian historian among them, consider that the mud of the Somme was worse even than that of Passchendaele the following year. To move one 18-pound gun twelve horses were needed. Sledges of corrugated iron were improvised. Vaguely defined infantry objectives were impossible to recognize. It was, in any case, often impossible to clamber out of the trenches, soldiers falling back in again over the slippery sides. Ladders had been used for fire-wood; so had wooden crosses from graves, and so had the large, tasteless ration biscuits. Matters were worsened by heavy fog, which when mingled with traces of gas and fumes from explosives, permanently affected men's lungs. Thousands were hauled away sick.

Those who were fifteen or twenty miles behind the front in the H.Q. châteaux had no idea of this state of affairs. Even the *Official History* admits:

No one who had not visited the front could really appreciate the state of exhaustion to which the troops were reduced owing to the rain and mud and the long distance over which all food, water and battle stores had to be carried ... the 2nd Worcestershires were up to the waist in slime.

It seems incredible now that men could have been asked to sally forth across a sea of mud for the sake of capturing a few more yards of it; at the time it must have appeared cruel madness. Nevertheless, 'stunts' were continually called for, and attempted.

As the weather grew colder there were many cases of frozen feet and frostbite. Duckboards sank into the mudfields, and the two or three mile journey through the back area became so terrible that relief battalions arrived at the front ill with exhaustion. Food was almost entirely cold (except for the tepid tea that was brought up in tins wrapped in straw). The commander of one Division (Major-General R. J. Pinney) stopped the issue of rum in his Division, as he had strong teetotal convictions (earlier on he had similarly forbade the use of steel helmets, believing that such modern contraptions would soften his troops). The Somme River itself froze two feet thick. Men committed suicide (the first and last dead men Robert Graves saw in France had shot themselves).

A. A. Hanbury-Sparrow, a Lieutenant-Colonel in the 8th Division, wrote in *The Land-Locked Lake*:

> It was impossible to move except on the duckboard tracks, and the weary trudge went on throughout the night. On either side of the track exhausted men of the oncoming division were lying slowly drowning in the mud. What could you do except give them the contents of your flask? For you must push, push on, with your men and get them to shelter somehow before they too collapsed. In the morning it was as if an epidemic of jaundice had broken out. The battalion was yellow with exhaustion.

Trench feet was rampant throughout the sector; often it resulted in amputation. Mark Plowman noted:

> He had a foot swollen to three times its normal size: a great shapeless bright pink lump. I shall be surprised if he doesn't lost that foot ... half a battalion being taken off in G.S. wagons because they are unable to walk. Many cannot even get into the wagons by themselves, and it is hard work carrying and lifting them in.

Somehow the sick and the wounded were carried back, covered from head to toe in mud, damp and glistening like seals. Edmund Blunden and others, write of the famous kneeling corpse near the Schwaben Redoubt, which had somehow remained in that position for weeks. It could be seen from some way off, a macabre monument to death on the old battlefield. Blunden was in the thick of this November nightmare. He describes men weeping as they struggled through the grey morass; of how the air was poisoned by rotting flesh; of how corpses were casually utilized for propping open doors; of how a man in his unit, half crazed, danced about in the mud nearly naked; of how the songs of the day, 'Take Me Back to Dear Old Blighty', 'When You're a Long, Long Way From Home', 'We Were Sailing Along on Moonlight Bay', drifted hopelessly across the wilderness. Men in the battalion next to his were in mud up to their armpits. Those who found them could not get them out. Their fate was not spoken of. Said the General, 'The air of Thiepval is most bracing.' But Blunden found it different:

Sluggish, soaking mists, or cold stinging wind, loaded the air and the spirit of man; the ruins of the world looked black and unalterable; Thiepval Wood's ghostly gallows-trees made no sound nor movement. The fog, dewing one's khaki, scarcely let the sun rise, and the grey chalky mud, as though to claim the only victory, crawled down the dug-out entrances, whether those still had stairs or were mere gullets, their woodwork burnt out by phosphorus bombs or shells. Where it had the chance, the mud filled these to the top.

Blunden was sent back, twelve miles behind the line, to see a new field oven in operation. A demonstration was shown – with sirloin.

The Surgeon-General, Sir Arthur Sloggett, in charge of all British medical services in France and Belgium, sent a horrified little note to Lord Northcliffe. 'I was out at Fricourt three days ago and I have *never* since the war commenced seen such mud – it is positively feet deep and horses and mules have been so bogged down that they have positively had to be shot.'

By now the artillery was even greater than at the beginning of the battle, illustrating one of the disadvantages that the British had been under in having to begin the offensive before all their preparations were complete. There were more than twice as many heavy guns in October as in July. But by now it was too late. British shell-fire merely turned over the mud around the German trenches, making them still more unapproachable. Robert Graves wrote of the kind of weapons that were now useful: 'Our primitive trench armoury included coshes, knuckle-dusters, home-made bombs extemporized from jam tins, and bayonets secured to broomsticks with surgical tape. I must admit that we never, in fact, used bows and arrows.'

Charteris went up one day quite close to the front, in the area which had been previously fought over, and discovered 'an awful scene of devastation'. Nevertheless, the General Staff in London was able to report in October to the War Committee that the enemy had 'been dealt a staggering blow from which he would find it very hard to recover'.

The soldiers had become a distant, quiet, cynical breed of men as far removed as they could possibly be from the cheerful Tommy of legend. Many of them had the old-soldier feeling; they were fighting with strangers; their former comrades were dead. As David Jones pointed out, the song of the Devons, 'We've lived and loved together', was all right for the Peninsular War, but it hardly applied now, when life was so short. The Somme was killing a lot of the old camaraderie in the British Army. The average soldier held the whole world in contempt – especially the staff, war correspondents, generals, and politicians. Wrote Plowman: 'I think with almost physical sickness of the legends that sustain our armchair patriots at home.' The main object in life, the only object, was to get away from the Somme, even, if necessary, by death.

Decorations were becoming meaningless. It was rumoured that decoration ribbons were 'dished out' by the Australians and the decision as to who should wear them was made by the toss of a coin.

Disillusioned young officers were shot for cowardice with gas-masks reversed over their heads. No doubt the executioners, themselves young officers and embittered soldiers, had no wish to look into the 'cowards' eyes as they shot them.

CHAPTER NINETEEN

RED TABS

WHILE thousands of British volunteers floundered about in the mud of the battlefront, miles behind the line a huge, costly organization arranged the supplies, the 'strategy', and the administration of the great army that was being almost dehumanized as winter advanced.

One of the major tasks of officers behind the line was the conducting of visitors around the sights. There was a continual stream of such visitors. Among newspaper proprietors, industrialists, and politicians, it was agreed that one was not informed on the war until one had visited the Somme Battle. In fact, of course, they never saw the battle. They were taken to the area of annihilation behind the lines. They saw wounded carried on stretchers. They were shown an old dug-out especially preserved for the purpose. They heard the guns. They dined in the châteaux, and discussed the progress of the war.

Haig, naturally, had a great number of visitors. He was a national figure, the hero of the day. It was an honour to lunch or dine with him at one of his various châteaux. On 7 October, he received a Japanese General. 'A most comic interview,' he noted. Mr. Balfour visited the battlefield and 'greatly enjoyed himself'. Haig wrote on this visit:

> After lunch we had a good talk. He [Balfour] seemed most pleased with all he had seen and was quite sure that our offensive in France should be supported to the utmost of our power. He told me that at one time he had favoured an effort in the Balkans, because he then thought the German front in France could not be pierced. Now our successes proved that his opinion was wrong.

Lloyd George visited the front again, and continued his double-face act with Haig, who wrote in a letter to his wife:

> I get on very well with Lloyd George, and yesterday he began to explain to me regarding his conversation with Foch, which I noted in my Diary. I would not let him go on with his explanation but merely said I had never paid the smallest attention to it.

It was not long before Northcliffe, who had to see everything, and who could hear the guns of the Somme from his country home, was at the battlefield, or not far from it. Arriving at G.H.Q., he asked for facilities for sending 'a direct and immediate' telegram to London. Charteris, who sent it over a special line, was astonished to find it was a message of love to Northcliffe's mother. The 'Chief', meeting Haig for the first time, noted his 'unusual facial angle, delicate features, strong chin; strong hands, no mysteries, no military swank, always at his maps and calculations'.

He made some notes:

A splendid day, a delightful garden, green and with a little winding pond; the roses and the sunshine are such a contrast to the bloody battle of the Somme so near this little château at Hesdin that I have been more melancholy and war-stricken than for many days past.

Northcliffe, whose better instincts were disgusted by the personal ambitions and plotting of the politicians at home, and who had a genuine sympathy with his 'public', part of which now found itself in such frightful conditions, was already completely on the side of Haig against the politicians, and their meeting strengthened this. 'He showed me his plans,' he wrote. 'Each time I see him I am convinced of his qualities. We talked of the wobble of the politicians.' He was taken to see a tank and, being of ample girth, on attempting to enter by the hole at the top got stuck half-way, and had to be extricated by being pulled by his legs from beneath while Wickham Steed, his faithful correspondent and companion, sat on his shoulders. According to Steed, getting him out of the tank again was an even harder task.

When he got back, Northcliffe wrote to Sir Philip Sassoon, Haig's private secretary:

You are dealing with people (politicians), some of whom are very thick-skinned, others very unscrupulous, but all of whom are afraid of newspapers. It is urgently necessary that they should be told, and more than once: 'Hands off the Army.' You may have noticed that directly the tanks were successful, Lloyd George issued a notice through the Press Bureau that they were due to Churchill. You will find that unless we watch these people they will claim that the great Battle of the Somme is due to the politicians.

As it turned out, that was the last thing the politicians wanted to claim. In his dislike of the politicians ('the slipperiness of eels, combined with the vanity of a professional beauty'), Northcliffe was blind to the failings of Haig.

At times Haig's published diary entries for this period seem one long list of those who lunched with him, and the nice things they said. There is hardly any mention of the mounting casualties or appalling conditions.

One of the strangest visitors to the front during the battle was the King of Montenegro, who was accompanied by a General in a shabby frock-coat who carried a small black bag from which he produced Montenegro medals – which he awarded to all who came within reach. The King, it was learned, had a reputation for borrowing money, which he forgot to repay.

Haig's intelligence chief, Charteris, took the main brunt of looking after the sightseers. He wrote in his diary:

> The stream of visitors is unending and takes up much valuable time. Yesterday we had a party comprising Lord Bryce, two Americans, and a Swede. Tomorrow we have the Prince of Monaco, who is said to be interested in nothing but zoology and biology.

An illuminating story recorded by Charteris gives some idea of the ignorance of civilians and staff alike about real conditions on the front. During the particularly bloody and horrible Australian stand at Pozières, while motoring behind the line, he 'overtook two young women on foot going the same way. I asked them what their destination was, and they said they wanted to walk to a unit in the front line and see what it was like to be under fire!' Charteris put them into a car going the other way and told them 'not to be naughty' in future.

The one man who visited the front and who could have done something to stop the misery was the Prime Minister himself. But he blithely looked at what he was shown, trusted what he heard, and, as always, hoped for the best. He told Haig that he was 'well pleased' at the way things were going. He was perhaps impressed most of all by Haig's old brandy, which was well known. Haig was somewhat mean with this, and he never sent it round more than once at a meal. After that it stood in grandeur in front of him. Asquith, according to Charteris, did not dare ask for another one. He brought his glass closer and closer to the bottle, and when this way failed he tried catching Haig's eye and then quickly glancing at the bottle. But all this did not affect the poker-faced cavalryman, and eventually, in desperation, the Prime Minister grabbed the bottle without a word and gulped down a glass. Haig later said: 'If he has not enough determination to ask for a glass of brandy when he wants it, he should not be Prime Minister.'

Another visitor to Haig, and a luncheon guest, was the new Minister of Munitions, Edwin Montagu, who had replaced Lloyd George – now War Minister and shortly (in December) to become Prime Minister. Noted Haig of Montagu: 'He is an agreeable man ... apparently a Jew.'

One of the few visitors to the Somme in the latter half of 1916 who suspected that all was not well, was H. G. Wells. Although he was capable of saying that the British helmets, in comparison to the French and German, were aesthetic crimes, he also noted the absurdities of the cavalry force. 'Behind our front at the time of my visit there were many thousands of cavalry, men tending horses, men engaged in transporting bulky fodder for horses and the like. These men were doing about as much in this war as if they had been at Timbuctoo.' While believing that the cavalry charge was as obsolete as the crossbow, Wells also imagined that rifles and bayonets were probably useless at the Somme, and he was not very wrong. He thought that more effective weapons would be knives, clubs, revolvers, knees, Roman swords, 'even the Zulu assegai'. He considered that warfare had reached 'Grade B2'.

Among the many activities going on behind the line was the production of the *Somme Times* by a group of officers in the Sherwood Foresters. In nostalgic, gay prose it made jokes about life at the front. It was a kind of Edwardian hangover, clinging on into a new world. It was as out of place at the Somme as would have been Marie Lloyd singing 'A little of what you fancy does you good' in a shelled dug-out.

There were rhymes by Gilbert Frankau ('The Nuts of the Old Brigade'), and R.C. Sherriff, and others fortunately anonymous.

> The Kaiser once said at Peronne
> That the Army we'd got was no bon,
> But between you and me
> He didn't compris
> The size of the job he had on.

There were fake advertisements ('at the Contalmaison

Opera House – the Original Bottle-nosed Comedian – Fritz –
in his new sketch: "I've Had Somme" '). There were jolly
little editorials: 'So here's to you all lads, the game is started,
keep the ball rolling and remember that the only good Hun is
a dead Hun.'

The dashing staff officers, with their red tabs, monocles,
swagger sticks, and superbly cut riding boots, were the men
who worked out the attacks taking place every day in the
waterlogged devastation of the front. Studying their maps with
rulers and pencils, they were often cavalrymen – to fit in
with the requirements of Haig and Gough. Lancers and Hussars still had social prestige in 1916; they were accustomed to
living well, and continued doing so through the course of the
battle. They dined and wined at each other's messes, they
entertained the French and were entertained by them, their
boots echoed in the polished halls of the great châteaux in
which they lived; they fished, they went for walks, and they
flirted with high-bred young French girls, who, said one, 'like
to get as near as they can'. Above all they went to Amiens,
the main city behind the British lines; and to Godbert's restaurant there. This establishment managed to put on night
after night quite outstanding menus, that would have delighted
the most demanding gourmet. It was considered by many
who visited it to have reached at this time exceptional culinary
heights. A certain staff officer who published (apparently at
his own expense) his diary under the title *The Salient, the
Somme and Arras* under the pseudonym of Bumble Bee, has
left an interesting record of this place. He was, at the time,
stationed at Baizieux ('not a bad little spot, as villages go in
these parts') and he wrote on 12 December:

Another miserable day – and another excellent lunch at
Godbert's. There is nothing cheap, nothing vulgar about
Godbert's. It does not stare you in the face aggressively like
the other hotels and restaurants do in the main thorough-
fares. You have to look for it before you find it in a peaceful
side street, standing well back and with a paved yard in
front for your car to be left in all security. A few steps lead
to a lobby where you may await friends and watch incomers.
At one end of the lobby is a cloakroom and at the other end
is the kitchen. But between kitchen and lobby, there is a
small office, where sits the Patronne, a business-like cheerful

little fat woman, with a number of little black curls up on her cranium. She inquires after your health and would like to know how many you will be for lunch, and where you want to sit. We always ask for Thérèse, but that is only because we are conservative in our habits and tastes. Having booked your table, you then proceed to fix up the menu with the Patronne and with the chef in the adjoining kitchen, if you are particular. Once your mind is made up about what you are going to eat, you may as well take things easily whilst they open the oysters and cook the chicken. You may wash your hands at leisure and improve your French with the fat girl in the cloakroom if she happens to be disengaged. The dining-hall is the finest in Amiens. It is made up of two long, lofty twin rooms with no other partition than arches between them. There are a number of small tables about and four waitresses, all of them young, dressed with care and taste, absolutely and unapproachably respectable, but fresh, refined, well-groomed and pleasant to look at. Thérèse, our choice, is bright, her hair is jet black, her skin is very white, her eyes very dark and full of fun, her hands a bit red, and her voice that of a siren. ... As soon as you have taken possession of the table allotted to you by the Patronne, old Henri sails up to you in a dignified way and makes his bow. He respectfully inquires what you have ordered for lunch so that he may recommend something suitable for you to drink. If you say 'oysters', he writes down 'Pouilly Fuissé'; if you expect a roast duck to follow he notes down 'Hermitage', says no more, but glides away to cool the white wine and to decant the red. Henri is the butler, and quite a character. ...

After lunch, back to staff problems.

The fighting troops at the front also had their moments off. The shell-shattered village of Meaulte, near the original front line of 1 July was one of their centres of relaxation. All around was a scene of desolation. There were few buildings left standing, but some of the original inhabitants had returned, and were living in rat-ridden cellars. They sold coffee, biscuits, and chocolate to troops caked in mud. A. D. Gristwood remembered 'a foul-mouthed, jostling throng that filled the streets, their pockets temporarily full and hearts light by reason of a week's respite. Small wonder drunkeness and debauchery ran riot in the place.'

CHAPTER TWENTY

THE ANCRE

On 9 November, when the troops thought the battle was over for the winter, the weather cleared, becoming dry and very cold. This seemed a good time to General Gough to make a last attempt on the German line. Why this attack was carried out so late in the year it is difficult to understand. There was no chance of a break-through, even Haig acknowledged that by now. One would have thought that attrition had had its fair share for one year, and that the two British armies would have been better employed busying themselves with winter preparations. But Haig agreed with the French to operate offensively during the winter to 'the utmost extent of my resources and opportunities, in order to hold the enemy's forces in our front, and to wear them down as much as possible'. There was shortly to be a conference at Chantilly to discuss the programme for 1917, and Haig wished to be in a strong position there. A success in the Somme sector would help him to get the French to agree that the main offensive of the year should again be left to the British (in the event, the French were only too willing to agree to this). On 12 November, he decided that an attack should be launched astride the Ancre, a tributory of the Somme, on Gough's part of the line. He reluctantly agreed that owing to the state of the ground the possibilities of the cavalry were somewhat limited, and most of them were withdrawn to comfortable winter quarters.

Gough had already ordered a barrage, which had been continuing for three days, and yet again Crown Prince Rupprecht made a note of the coming attack. This sector of the front had resisted all attempts since 1 July, and would probably have done so on 13 November if there had not been thick fog, restricting visibility to thirty yards. Although they were disorganized, many of the British troops arrived in the German trenches before the enemy were aware what was happening. Heavy hand-to-hand fighting ensued in the muddy trenches and around the deep dug-outs in which the Germans had successfully sheltered during the bombardment (among other refinements, they were equipped with electric alarm bells).

Fighting continued for the next five days and some small advance was made, the Fifth Army suffering heavy casualities. It was bitterly cold; the temperatures mostly below freezing point. The ruined villages of Beaumont Hamel and Beaucourt were taken, but farther north the attack on Serre had to be abandoned. The Royal Naval Division, after much confusion, made good headway in small bands of men, one of which was commanded by Lieutenant-Colonel B. C. Freyberg (later Lord Freyberg) who, despite being wounded several times, continued leading his men towards a formidable redoubt and through wire that had been hardly touched by the barrage. Freyberg's battalion, which had pushed up the bank of the river for two miles, had to wait twenty-four hours until their own artillery ceased firing in front of them. Freyberg, often considered the greatest individual hero of the Battle of the Somme, was awarded the V.C.

Throughout the offensive on the Ancre it had been misty and cold, with a thin drizzle. The mud was almost impassable around the German trenches, where the quagmire had been stirred up by the bombardment. The conditions in which the action was fought have probably never been equalled in infantry warfare. On the night of the 17th snow fell for the first time, and on the 18th there was a blizzard. The action on the Ancre resulted in a German salient being captured; but from a defensive point of view the line which Gough's Army was now obliged to hold during the following months was an even poorer one than the line out of which they had struggled. Having at last won the crest of the ridge, the advantage had been thrown away by advancing into the depression beyond. Ludendorff noted that the Ancre Battle, 'in spite of the enemy's great expenditure of men, ended on the whole favourably for us'.

CHAPTER TWENTY-ONE

THE ALLIES AND THE ENEMY

DURING the Somme offensive the French confined their efforts to rounding out the advance that the British were making to the north, and protecting the British right flank. In September, Fayolle's Sixth Army was joined in the battle by Micheler's Tenth Army on its right wing. A persistent and bloody, but unspectacular, advance was made. In the end they succeeded in taking a slightly greater acreage of mud from the Germans than did the British, with considerably less cost. They concealed their intentions well, their field organization was good, their soldiers were experienced. Nevertheless, they suffered casualties of nearly a quarter of a million (some authorities say considerably more), inflicting about the same number on the Germans. Although the pressure on Verdun had been relieved, little had been done to soothe the wave of discontent that had been sweeping France since the beginning of the year, especially in the army. Scapegoats had to be found, and at long last the French politicians felt strong enough to stand up to 'Papa' Joffre, and he was replaced by General Nivelle. Joffre blamed failure on the British, for calling off the battle too soon. If they had persevered during the winter, he said, victory could have been won. Foch, somewhat unjustly, fell with him, but only temporarily. Although he had reached the age limit of sixty-five for the active list at the end of September, he had at that time been kept on. But then it was decided that he, too, would have to go, and he was pronounced unfit for duty on medical grounds (earlier in the year he had been in a car accident; believing that all loss of time was sinful, he held the view that his car could not possibly be driven too fast). Considering that he had from the first been an opponent of the whole idea of the Somme, he was, understandably, most indignant at his removal.

Throughout the battle the Germans had been fighting a rearguard action; first, under Falkenhayn, to preserve every inch of ground from falling into the hands of the allies, and then, under Ludendorff, to give time while a completely new line was built miles to the rear. The conditions in which the

Germans did, in fact, accomplish this latter feat were wretched in the extreme. The Somme was known to them as the 'Bath of Blood'. Military police formed cordons around the railway stations at Bruges and Lille so that civilians could not see the streams of wounded pouring back. Troops being relieved were forced to sing in the trains. Their rations were considerably less than those of the allied troops, and they suffered tortures from thirst. They were supplied with bottled water, the stores of which were frequently hit by shells. Troops were reduced to drinking out of shell craters. There was a great deal of sickness among the Germans; the decomposing bodies of the fallen before their positions poisoned the air. Bavarians quarrelled with Prussians, each saying the others were not playing their part. Letters from home about 'millionaires and bloated aristocrats' infuriated them. Many suffered from shell-shock, with blank, staring eyes and trembling mouths. One of them wrote after a spell in the line: 'A handful of half-mad wretched creatures, worn-out in body and in mind, were all that was left of our battalion.' In the second half of the battle their casualties were probably as great as those of the British, and deserters started going over, a thing almost unknown before.

The tough, unimaginative Falkenhayn was replaced by the Hindenburg-Ludendorff partnership on 29 August. Although Hindenburg was officially the Commander-in-Chief and Ludendorff the equivalent of Chief-of-Staff, the two had joint responsibility for all the decisions. On 5 September, they visited the Western Front for the first time, having spent practically all the war so far in the east. The change-over was actually made on the Eastern Front, Falkenhayn having been unimpressed enough with the allied efforts at the Somme to move to what seemed the more important sector. There they met, with other commanders, Crown Prince Rupprecht, who told them that he was delighted the Verdun offensive had been forced to stop – a thing he had always wanted. Ludendorff agreed that Verdun 'should have been called off immediately it assumed the character of a battle of attrition. The gain no longer justified the losses.'

In his memoirs, Ludendorff wrote of the Somme: 'The loss of ground up to date appeared to me of little importance in itself.' He soon saw that the bitter fighting had 'made the most extraordinary demands both on commanders and troops. The troops were getting exhausted'. He did his best to alleviate the suffering. He got divisions out of the line before the point of utter collapse. He did not insist on the retention of all ground; in fact, he insisted that the line should be flexible. He was not greatly concerned about the great fortresses that had been lost, considering them too clumsy. He preferred a less conspicuous line of light trenches, which could be abandoned without great loss if it were advantageous to do so, and this was what the Germans had after the loss of their first and second systems. He also considered that the German soldier was beginning to forget how to shoot. If he were a better rifleman, then much hand-to-hand fighting would be unnecessary, he thought. Ludendorff, a brilliant general by World War 1 standards, admitted after the war that German losses on the Somme had been very heavy, even under his command. The exact figure is uncertain, but they were probably just less than half a million. Let us, however, leave the last word on the German side to Falkenhayn.

The clever propaganda of the entente, which unfortunately was making itself felt within the [German] Empire, has made out the Battle of the Somme to be a serious disaster for Germany. It is true our losses were very heavy. In reality, however, it had comparatively little influence on the further course of the war, in no way proportionate to the sacrifices of the entente.

CHAPTER TWENTY-TWO

'TOMMY ATKINS'

A KIND of legend about the Battle of the Somme, and the men who were fighting it, was built up at home. This was done through press reports by correspondents who never saw the real front, by authors who were sent out especially to write books that would add to this legend, and by the unwillingness of the public to believe anything unpleasant. The picture of the soldier at the Somme, was of a gay, facetious, careless soldier, facing all odds with a grin and confounding the Germans with his indefatigable lightheartedness. His name was Tommy Atkins from Boer War days, and he was the sort of brave Britisher who cockily said: ' 'Arf a mo', Kaiser,' as he lit up a fag in a lull in the fighting.

As the battle wore on, the space it occupied in the Press got less and less. The correspondents, hampered by censorship and red tape, knew practically nothing; they could report practically nothing. The technique of human stories was not yet fully developed. Reports became negative, and almost meaningless. 'A month of Minor Attacks.' 'Splendid Spirit of all Arms.' An example of the kind of thing which appeared nearly every day was: 'Our attacks were local and made with a few battalions with the object of gaining more advanced trenches at three points so as to improve our front line.' The newspapers began to forget about Haig's armies at the Somme; there were more interesting despatches to feature from the east. H. P. Robinson of *The Times* tried to give some impression of the horror of the November battlefield, a thing which he himself only half understood. He was addicted to referring to the troops as 'stout fellows'. Philip Gibbs also attempted to convey some idea of conditions. His speciality was in reporting the German side of the story, which he gathered from prisoners. His reports naturally always reflected how badly things were going for the Hun.

Among the journalists who visited the front were St. Loe Strachey, editor of the *Spectator*. Said Haig: 'He seemed much pleased with everything.' The editor of the *Morning Post*, Gwynne, dined and stayed the night with Haig ('like most newspaper men, is very self-satisfied and talks as if he rules the universe'). J. A. Spender of the *Westminster Gazette*, on the other hand, found favour - 'an honest patriot'.

Within twelve months four observers had written books on the Somme, at least one of which was aimed specifically at the American propaganda market. They were all almost identical, being mainly constructed from official reports. The Battle of the Somme had been a great British victory, they said. Robinson and Gibbs wrote two of these books. The one published only in America was by John Buchan. Like Haig, he had been at B.N.C., Oxford, and was a Scot. He helped Haig in his reports (these are, in fact, remarkably well written, and subtle in making disaster look like victory; in contrast to Haig's unaided writings). The best of the four books was by John Masefield. ('He is a poet, but I am told he has written the best account of the British landing in Gallipoli.')

Another book, rather different, was actually published in 1916. This was *Somme Battle Stories,* illustrated by that master of humbug Bruce Bairnsfather. It consisted of first-hand accounts of the battle told to Captain A. J. Dawson, whose task it was to meet returning hospital ships and interview the wounded. Every man was a hero; every man had a grand tale to tell. Loaded with sentimentality, it sold excellently. The battle it told of was a kind of football match.

> With matches, or scraps of paper, or a nicotine-stained forefinger made to serve as pencil in the nearest conveniently dusty surface, they will give you elaborate expositions of the tactics they have helped to work out ... and their lovable faces sometimes show a glimmer of disappointment, for that one does not take copious notes regarding these demonstrations.

This is what they allegedly told Dawson:

> Oh, I say, you know, don't bother about that guff. Eh? Oh, just an ordinary front line trench you know, rather chipped about, of course, by the Boche heavies, you know. My chaps were all in splendid heart, and keen as mustard to get the word 'Go!' I was lucky; met my friend G——. He took me along to his dug-out, after I'd got all my chaps in position, and gave me some jolly good hot café-au-lait. The weather was jolly just then; but there'd been a lot of rain, and the trench was in a beastly state.

Said another:

This business of fighting – fighting continuously and cheerily in the presence of devastating casualties – has a good deal in common with swimming and bicycling and things of that sort in which instinct plays a big part; and horse-riding too.

Dawson's book is packed with this kind of propaganda.

People who try to measure the importance of the Push by the ground gained or even by the casualties inflicted, will fall a long way short in their estimate of what it all means. In my opinion, what's been accomplished this month would have been a big gain to the Allies if our casualties had been five times what they have been.

A wounded Irish lieutenant was reported by Dawson thus:

The business of this Push is too big for letters. Bedad, it's too big for literature itself ... it's an assertion of the bed-rock decency and goodness of our people, and I wouldn't have missed it, not for all the gold in London town.

And, of course, Dawson had to have the views of a Cockney:

Fed up? Wot, ahr boys fed up, sir? Not likely? Wy, we're just beginnin' to like it. But I bet Mr. Boche is gettin' a bit fed up.... To 'ear the way they talks abaht that Devil's Wood, you'd think there was something wrong abaht the bloomin' plice ... wy, you couldn't 've asked fer a nicer plice for a scrap. Wot do I think uv Mr. Boche? Oh, 'e's orlright once yet get ter know 'is little tricks – the blighter.

This last remark is a true reflection of feeling at the front. There was a kind of sympathy between the Germans and the British. They felt that they were all victims together of some inevitable force; in a trap that no one who had not entered could ever understand. Witness this letter of F. H. Keeling:

I respect the Germans as soldiers, I sympathize with the poor devil of a German infantryman who goes through the same hell as I do in a bombardment, and I see the German point of view about the *Lusitania* and the Cavell business and other matters too clearly for the yap, yap, yap of the Press about these things.

The record of the Press during the Battle of the Somme is a disgraceful one. Although they were fed with official mumbo-jumbo, they seemed content with it. As a whole the Press was blind to the truths of the battle, and it failed in its responsibilities.

But as the casualty lists grew, and as the meagre effects of dead soldiers found their way home, and as more and more tattered, blood-stained uniforms (often also sent home) were buried in thousands of back-gardens, people began to wonder.

Not quite everyone was hoodwinked, and one of those who had never ceased to wonder, right from the beginning, was Winston Churchill. As early as 1 August 1916, he sent a remarkable memorandum to F. E. Smith, Attorney-General and a member of the Cabinet. In it he said:

> We are not making for any point of strategic or political consequence. Verdun at least would be a trophy – to which sentiment on both sides has become mistakenly attached.
> But what are Peronne and Bapaume, even if we were likely to take them? The open country towards which we are struggling by inches is capable of entrenched defence at every step, and is utterly devoid of military significance. There is no question of breaking the line, of 'letting loose the cavalry in the open country behind', or of inducing a general withdrawal of the German armies in the West.

Churchill's memorandum was circulated in the Cabinet by Smith, and was even read by the King, but nothing came of it. Neither Asquith, had he wanted to, nor Lloyd George, who did, were in a powerful enough position to remove Haig, with the mass of the country and popular opinion behind him. With Allenby yet to prove himself, there seemed, in any case, no one better. But the politicians had let the generals get the better of them; insidiously, their authority had been undermined. A quarter of a century later Churchill had not forgotten, and he did not make the same mistake as they had done.

CHAPTER TWENTY-THREE

'NAPOO!'

THE Battle of the Somme officially ended on 18 November 1916, in the blizzards and snow of the Ancre. The show was, in the army expression, 'napoo'. For the first time in modern history Britain had been forced to abandon its traditional policy of siding with a powerful continental ally and relying on a small professional army to make its contribution. It had fought a great continental power almost on its own. Was it a victory? Or was it a disaster? No one seemed to know.

The process of clearing the battlefield was begun. Burial parties worked hard for several months, using dumps of quick-lime – as German shelling frequently uncovered bodies. Whole divisions undertook salvage work. Equipment, clothing and stores of every description were littered over the battlefield. All this was gathered in great dumps. Some divisions managed partially to re-equip themselves from salvaged equipment.

Lloyd George got his premiership at last, after some extraordinarily involved plotting by himself, Bonar Law, and Sir Maxwell Aitken (later Lord Beaverbrook). Asquith, broken by the death of his son, retired from the limelight.

Douglas Haig went on leave on 22 November. He saw the new house his wife Dorothy had bought on Kingston Hill. She later wrote:

> Douglas was quite delighted with it. We managed to play a round or two of golf at Coombe Hill and at Sunningdale and we both enjoyed our games. The weather was lovely. On our way back from Sunningdale we called on Lord Derby at Cotworth Park.

(In the beginning of September, Lady Haig had written asking Haig to come home for a few days 'whilst the children and I are still at Deal, on holiday.)

Before he went on leave Haig had met Joffre at their scheduled conference at Chantilly to discuss the 1917 campaign. They agreed that there should be a further offensive on the Somme early in the year; and the main share of the attack should fall to the British. In fact, they should do exactly the same as they had done in 1916. But Joffre fell from his throne, and the plan was revised.

On 23rd December Haig sent his final dispatch on the Somme. In it he made the statement: 'Machine-guns play a great part – almost a decisive part under some conditions – in modern war.' Despite this discovery he sent thousands more to their deaths in hopeless advances against German machine-guns in 1917 on the Ypres Salient. But from now on, at least, he received less new troops from home – a notable victory for Lloyd George.

By now the Germans were beginning to think longingly of of peace. If Haig kept on battering at them for years, he likely would win the war – even if he killed practically every adult male in Britain doing so. The Kaiser couldn't ignore the possibility. President Wilson, of the United States, asked the belligerents to define their war aims, and to allow him to negotiate a reasonable peace. But even Lloyd George was horrified at this. The Hun had to be destroyed by a 'Knock-Out Blow'. That was why Britain was at war ... wasn't it?

For years the argument has continued over the Somme. Haig's supporters maintain it saved the front from collapse when Verdun and France were threatened; that it weakened the German army so that it was never the same force again. His detractors have said that the German army did well enough in 1918, that the battle weakened the British army more than it did the German; that it was a pointless slaughter. They point out that, although perhaps delayed, it would have occurred whether the Germans attacked Verdun or not. Haig's defenders have always been strong. Mostly military men, some of them ex-staff officers, they appeared at times something like an unorganized conspiracy to protect his reputation. They realize that the present decade is a vital one in the final assessment of the man; that the present judgement is likely to be the one handed down to history. Their books and articles are coming fast one on the other.

It was not, of course, Haig's fault that he had grave shortcomings as a military commander; it was the fault of a society that put him, the man he was, in the position it did. But it is not easy to forgive his refusal to see his errors, his lack of contact with his fighting men, and his blind rush into the mud of Passchendaele in 1917 as if nothing but success had come from similar methods at the Somme.

Some people, however, had learnt a deep lesson. The young commanders who had seen what trench warfare was like would be affected by the memory for the rest of their days. In 1939, Archibald Wavell said in his famous Cambridge lectures that he believed in the individual use of the infantryman. To move men into battle in long waves as Haig had done at the Somme was to sanction mass butchery. And Montgomery wrote: 'The frightful casualties appalled me. The so-called "good fighting generals" of the war appeared to me to be those who had a complete disregard for human life.' After the invasion of Normandy, in another war, Eisenhower wished to continue through France in a long, straight line, whereas Montgomery begged to be allowed to go forward in one powerful thrust. Montgomery knew about the Somme; the American didn't. In the 1930s Clement Atlee was all against conscription; he, too, had fought in the trenches. 'In World War I,' he said, 'the generals had too many men, and they didn't use their brains. They didn't have to.'

It is unlikely that anyone will ever know exactly how many men were killed, wounded, or captured at the Battle of the Somme. Figures were successfully falsified by both sides at the time, for propaganda purposes – so successfully, in fact, that it is now only possible to guess at the real ones. Thus, for years practically every military writer has given a different figure.

The Adjutant-General at G.H.Q. put all British casualties for 1916 on the Western Front at 607,784, and Sir Charles Oman, who was in charge of investigating the enemy's casualty returns (which were particularly evasive) afterwards said that losses at the Somme had been 'about exactly the same' for both sides – five hundred and sixty thousand.

J. E. Edmonds, the Official Historian, put them (in 1931) at six hundred thousand; the British *and* French just below, the Germans just above. But after the publication of the *Official German History of the War*, which said there were 'about' five hundred thousand German casualties at the Somme, he put the German figure up to six hundred and eighty thousand, with evident relief, by pointing out various deficiencies in the German figures. It is important to remember, however, that the Germans were anxious to show, in their account of the battle, how their infantry only gave ground after suffering immense losses.

The official Allied figures are 419,654 British and 204,253

French. The reliability of these figures can be be judged by the fact that the French were not finally corrected until 1936.

Haig himself said that it was 'beyond doubt' that the German losses were 'very considerably higher' than those of the allies. But J. H. Boraston, who was a member of Haig's staff and who was concerned with the drafting of the official communiques (and an ardent, almost fanatical, admirer of Haig's), put the British losses at four hundred and ten thousand, and the German at only one hundred and eighty thousand. The latter figure is from a 'calculation of German returns made available since the Armistice'. The Australians also put the British losses at twice as high as the German. So did Lloyd George. The French writer, Girard, estimated German losses at three hundred and seventy-three thousand and allied at five hundred thousand. But some writers in recent years have continued to give the impression that German losses were in excess of those of the allies, *but no really reliable figures exist*. The exact figures of how many men were killed and maimed at the Battle of the Somme will never be known – but the British dead and injured must have been over a quarter of a million, the heart of a whole generation. The reward was an advance of nowhere more than eight miles, in the direction of the Push, along a front of twelve miles. From all three countries taking part, about three million fought at the Somme, of whom about one million were casualties. Of the British divisions in France in 1916 fifty-three took part in the Somme battle, including four from Canada, four from Australia, and one from New Zealand. Twenty French divisions took part.

On 6 September 1916 Ludendorff decided to retreat from the Somme, whether the allies continued their offensive there or not, in order to shorten his line. The new line, planned with due regard to experience gained in the battle, was duly constructed; it was completed during the winter. By the Germans it was known as the 'Siegfried Line', by the British as the 'Hindenburg Line'. It took three months to construct, and shortened the German front by thirty-two miles. During March 1917, they quietly retreated to it, incurring negligible losses in the process. In some cases it was days before the Allies, the French especially, were convinced that the trenches opposite them were practically deserted. Haig sent his cavalry after them, but they got stuck in the quagmire, and there was an extraordinary state of confusion as traffic became congested on the battered roads and all telephonic communications ceased

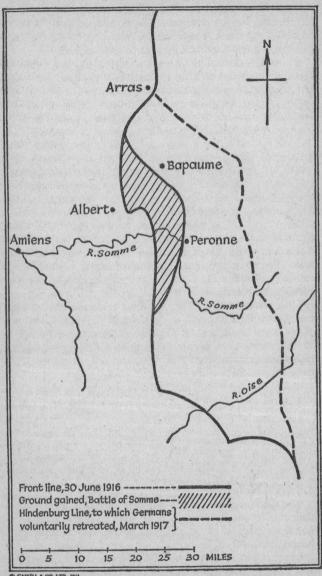

N

Arras •

• Bapaume

Albert •

Amiens •

R. Somme

• Peronne

R. Somme

R. Oise

Front line, 30 June 1916 ------------
Ground gained, Battle of Somme --- ////////////
Hindenburg Line, to which Germans }
voluntarily retreated, March 1917 } ------

```
0    5    10    15    20    25    30  MILES
```

© CASSELL & CO. LTD. 1961

to exist. In some areas the obliteration the Germans left behind was so complete that it was difficult to locate positions. All hope of catching the retreating enemy before he reached the Hindenburg Line had to be abandoned.

Many treasures of art were removed from the evacuated zone by the Germans. Most of the population were evacuated, but small groups were left behind with rations for two or three days. Most of the young girls were taken away. Ludendorff did not want to leave too many recruits and labourers, but he was also anxious to embarrass the allied food supplies.

The area the allied troops entered was a booby-trap nightmare land, with a strange air of unreality and danger. Trees at the side of the roads were three-quarters sawn through; gusts of wind bowled them over on top of passing traffic. Hidden land mines were timed to go off up to forty days later. They inflicted many casualties; as when the Town Hall at Bapaume blew up a week after it had been occupied, killing two French Deputies and some Australians who were sleeping there. Tempting bits of equipment set off a dozen grenades when they were picked up. Trip wires drawn across dug-out entrances would send the unwary flying inside and set off a bomb to bury them alive.

Wells were poisoned. The burning town of St. Quentin lit up the night sky for many miles. The Germans had achieved one of the most thorough and destructive laying-wastes of history. In villages that had been carefully torn down by hand, every house was obliterated. Bridges were mined, roads made impassable, orchards destroyed. Wrote Ludendorff:

We were now more compactly and firmly established than we had been along our previous extended line. The tactical measures of the enemy had been frustrated. He was no longer able to attack in the same directions as before. The country we had left was devastated, and before military operations could be made possible upon it a certain amount of restoration was essential. We had completely achieved the objects we had in view.

The Germans had in fact nullified the small dent made in their line by the British armies. In their advance in 1918 they got it all back anyhow, and just passed Albert (the British having done very little defence work after the Somme).

But the Americans arrived, the German civilian population was hungry, and there was civil war in Berlin. Nearly a million

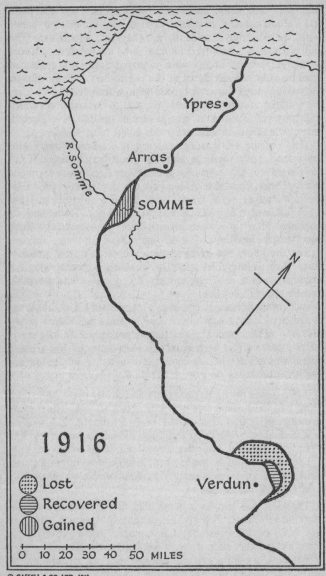

Ypres •

R. Somme

Arras •

SOMME

N

1916

Lost
Recovered
Gained

Verdun •

0 10 20 30 40 50 MILES

© CASSELL & CO. LTD. 1961

men from Britain and the Empire had died. The war was over, and Haig had won it, or so most people said. In 1918 he turned down a viscountcy; in 1919 he accepted an earldom. The man they had nicknamed 'Lucky' was awarded a hundred thousand pounds, and given a country house and estate at Bemersyde, where he lived, as he had wished, in 'the manner to which I am accustomed'. He spent a large part of his remaining days in the interest of and care of the survivors of his gallant army, which had always obeyed his every command, many of whom remain loyal to his memory to this day.

Happy days were here again, roses bloomed in Picardy, and the remains of the regular Army sighed with relief and got back to the business of peace, and did its best to forget the nightmare it had recently experienced. One officer was heard to exclaim on Armistice Day: 'Thank God we can now get back to real soldiering.' The cavalry kept in command of things, and the horses came back into their own, and the tanks were almost discarded.

And gradually the grass sprouted, the trees grew, the farmers toiled in the filthy waste, discovering as many as half a dozen corpses a day ten years later, and the birds returned, and the woods lived again, and men fished on the banks of the sleepy Somme, and lovers walked hand in hand through the orchards of Bazentin. And sometimes quiet Englishmen would visit this balmy countryside, in the summer, and still do, singly and in small groups. They do not speak much; but wander down the lanes and across the gentle hills, as if they are looking for something. As they gaze across the peaceful scene only they are able to hear the screaming of shells overhead, the thunder of explosions, and the groans of the wounded; to smell the fumes and the stench and the mist; and to feel the damp and the misery in their bones.

BIBLIOGRAPHY

The following have been especially useful:

Official History of the War, Military Operations, France and Belgium, 1916 (Macmillan, 1932 and 1938)

Despatches 1915-1919, Douglas Haig; ed. J. H. Boraston (Dent, 1919)

Private Papers of Douglas Haig; ed. R. Blake (Eyre & Spottiswoode, 1952)

The World Crisis, Winston Churchill (New ed., Odhams, 1938)

War Memoirs, David Lloyd George (New ed., Odhams, 1938)

Sir Douglas Haig's Command, G. A. B. Dewar and J. H. Boraston (Constable, 1922)

Haig, Duff Cooper (Faber, 1935)

The Man I Knew, Dorothy Countess Haig (Moray Press, 1938)

Haig, Sir George Arthur (Heinemann, 1928)

Soldiers and Statesmen, Field Marshal Sir William Robertson (Cassell, 1926)

Allenby, Field Marshal Lord Wavell (Harrop, 1946)

Life of Lord Rawlinson of Trent, Maj.-General Sir Frederick Maurice (Cassell, 1928)

Soldiering On, General Sir Hubert Gough (Barker, 1954)

At G.H.Q., Brig.-General John Charteris (Cassell, 1931)

Memories and Reflections, Lord Asquith (Cassell, 1928)

Northcliffe, R. Pound and G. Harmsworth (Cassell, 1959)

Kitchener, Sir Philip Magnus (John Murray, 1958)

Winston Churchill, Virginia Cowles (Hamish Hamilton, 1953)

My Brother and I, William George (Eyre & Spottiswoode, 1958)

Reputations, Capt. B. H. Liddell Hart (John Murray, 1928)

Memoirs, Marshal Joffre (Geoffrey Bles, 1932)

Foch, A. H. Atteridge (Skeffington, 1919)

Foch, Sir George Aston (Hutchinson, 1929)

Foch, Capt. B. H. Liddell Hart, (Eyre & Spottiswoode, 1931)

Verdun, Marshal Pétain (E. Mathews & Marrot, 1930)

General Headquarters 1914-1916, General Falkenhayn (Hutchinson, 1919)

My War Memories, General Erich Ludendorff (Hutchinson, 1919)

Prelude to Victory, Maj.-General Sir Edward Spears (Cape, 1939)

History of the Great War, C. R. M. F. Cruttwell (Oxford, 1934)

The Tanks, Capt. B. H. Liddell Hart (Cassell, 1959)

The Canadians in France, Lieut.-Colonel H. Steele (Fisher Unwin, 1920)

The Fifth Army, General Sir Hubert Gough (Hodder & Stoughton, 1931)

Anzac to Amiens, C. E. W. Bean (Australian War Memorial, 1946)

The Battles of the Somme, Philip Gibbs (Heinemann, 1917)

The Germans on the Somme, Philip Gibbs (Darling, 1917)

The Battle of the Somme, John Buchan (New York, 1917)

The Old Front Line, John Masefield (Heinemann, 1917)

The Battle of the Somme, John Masefield (Heinemann, 1919)

The Turning Point, Sir H. P. Robinson (Heinemann, 1917)

Haig's Great Push, H. N. Williams (Hutchinson, 1917)

Somme 1916, E. Kabisch (Berlin, 1937)

La Bataille de la Somme, G. Girard (Paris, 1937)

Gallant Gentlemen, E. S. Turner (Michael Joseph, 1956)

Somme Battle Stories, Capt. A. J. Dawson (Hodder & Stoughton, 1916)

The Somme, and the Coward, A. D. Gristwood (Cape, 1927)

The Irish on the Somme, M. Macdonagh (Hodder & Stoughton, 1917)

Memoirs of an Infantry Officer, Siegfried Sassoon (Faber, 1930)

Goodbye to All That, Robert Graves (New ed., Cassell, 1957)

A Subaltern's War, Charles Edmonds (Peter Davies, 1929)

A Subaltern on the Somme, 'Mark VII' (Dent, 1927)

Undertones of War, Edmund Blunden (Cobden-Sanderson, 1928)

Carrying On, Ian Hay (Blackwood, 1917)

Memories of Delville Wood, J. A. Lawson (Cape Town, 1918)

Twelve Days, S. Rogerson (Arthur Barker, 1933)

The Golden Virgin, Henry Williamson (Macdonald, 1957)

The Men I Killed, Brig.-General Crozier (Michael Joseph, 1937)

Up to Mametz, L. W. Griffith (Faber, 1931)

Going Across, letters and diary of Lieut. M. St. H. Evans; ed. F. Delamain (R. H. Johns, Newport, 1952)

Newspapers of the period

NOTES

I MAKE no apology for the large number of quotations in this book. Many are descriptive; many of the battlefront. They were mostly written by men who were there. Publishers and dates are given only for books not mentioned in the Bibliography.

The opening quotation is from *Sir Douglas Haig's Command* by J. H. Boraston and G. A. B. Dewar.

PROLOGUE. Compiled after consulting the many first-hand accounts of 1 July, and talking to survivors.

CHAPTER 1. There is an excellent description of the Somme valley before the war in the Introduction to *The Somme, and the Coward*. Another colourful description is Cruttwell's history. A detailed topographical and geological study is in D. W. Johnson's *Battlefields of the World War* (American Geographical Society, New York, 1921).

Accounts of the giddy life of pre-war army officers can be found in *My Early Life* by Winston Churchill (Butterworth, 1930), and especially in Osbert Sitwell's *Great Morning* (Macmillan, 1948), which gives a fascinating picture of the extraordinary state of affairs that existed right up to the eve of the war. E. S. Turner's *Gallant Gentlemen* was also very useful, as was Wavell's chapter in the *New Cambridge Modern History*, Vol. XII (1960). Lord Birdwood's remark is from *Khaki and Gown* (Ward Locke, 1941). *England in the Nineteenth Century* by David Thomson (Penguin, 1950), *British History in the Nineteenth Century and After* by G. M. Trevelyan (Longmans, 1937), and the *Dictionary of National Biography*, were consulted, among others, for the historical background. For the short resumé of the war, as it concerned the Western Front before the Somme battle, *History of the World War* by J. E. Edmonds (Oxford, 1951), the official historian of the war, was useful. *1914* by James Cameron (Cassell, 1959) gives an excellent summary of the start of the war. The relevant entry in *Encyclopaedia Britannica*, contributed by Capt. B. H. Liddell Hart, was also helpful. Asquith's letter if from Haig's *Private Papers* (p. 116).

CHAPTER 2. Joffre's *Memoirs*. Charteris's *At G.H.Q.* (quotations from pp. 136, 138, and for the Invalides story). Robertson's *Soldiers and Statesmen*. The *Official History* (Vol. I quoted). Churchill's comment is from *The World Crisis* (p. 1070); D. C. Somervell's from *The Reign of King George V* (Faber, 1935 ; p. 146).

Countess Haig's book gives the most intimate picture of Haig's early days, and it makes better reading than Duff Cooper's loyal, straightforward biography. There is an interesting pen-portrait of Haig in Liddell Hart's *Reputations*. Haig's *Cavalry Studies* (Hugh Rees, 1907) is available at the British Museum Library ; it is not recommended for light reading. The 'paper' on cavalry is mentioned in Cooper. The failings in Haig's character, as revealed in his subsequent career, are recorded in *Men and Power* by Lord Beaverbrook (Hutchinson, 1956), as is his influence at Buckingham Palace. Haig's remarks on French are from the *Private Papers* (pp. 109, 108, 121). These papers, consisting mainly of entries in his diary and letters to his wife, are cruelly revealing of the man, and are indispensable to study of the First World War.

CHAPTER 3. The three biographies of Foch mentioned in the Bibliography. Joffre's *Memoirs* and Pétain's *Verdun* (both quoted) give vivid, personal views of the battle for Verdun. The remark of des Vallières is from *Haig: Master of the Field* by Maj.-Gen. Sir John Davidson (P. Nevill, 1953 ; p. 4). Falkenhayn's *General Headquarters* and Haig's *Private Papers* (quoted from p. 125, and for Joffre's remark about the state of the French army from p. 145).

CHAPTER 4. Churchill's *World Crisis* and Lloyd George's *War Memoirs* (the Balfour quotation from p. 322) give full-blooded, one-sided accounts of the bickering between the military and the politicians. Also Cowles's *Churchill*, Magnus's *Kitchener*, Robertson's *Soldiers and Statesmen*, the Northcliffe biography, and Haig's *Private Papers* – from which Lloyd George's and Robertson's letters are quoted (pp. 128, 122). There are succinct pictures of Asquith and Robertson in *Men and Power*. Magnus's biography of *Kitchener* probably gives a fairer view of the man than does that of Sir George Arthur (Kitchener's private secretary) (Macmillan, 1920), and it is this that has been mainly used for the assessment given here. *Politicians and the War* (Oldbourne, 1960) by Lord Beaverbrook gives an inside picture of the political intrigue before and during the battle.

CHAPTER 5. *The Old Front Line* by John Masefield, an official observer, gives a very detailed description of the positions before 1 July. H. G. Wells wrote of the back area in vivid journalistic style, after a short visit, in *The War and the Future* (Cassell, 1917). Cruttwell's history, and Buchan's *The Battle of the Somme* were also particularly helpful.

CHAPTER 6. Haig's *Private Papers* (quotations from pp. 146, 147, 148, 149, 150). Liddell Hart's *Reputations* gives a frank account of the differences between Haig and Rawlinson. *At G.H.Q.* by Charteris (quotation from p. 151). The *Official History* (the important quotation concerning Rawlinson's doubts is from p. 252). Maurice's biography of Rawlinson; the latter's seven objections to Haig's plan are from p. 155. Wavell's magnificent biography of Allenby. The *Dictionary of National Biography* gives some useful information on the clashes of the careers of the two Generals. The biographies of Foch were again useful. I have extracted Haig's words about Divine help from Leon Wolff's *In Flanders Fields* (Longmans, 1959).

CHAPTER 7. Magnus and Sir George Arthur (*op. cit.*) for Kitchener's Army. Churchill's memo to Asquith is from *The World Crisis* (p. 502). *Gallant Gentlemen* for training at home (French's words from p. 276). Sassoon's *Memoirs of a Fox-Hunting Man* (Faber, 1928), and *The Golden Virgin* (quoted from p. 223) for the march to the front; there is also a good account of Étaples in the latter. Robert Graves served in the line before the battle, and I am grateful to *Goodbye to All That* (quotations from pp. 171, 170), and there is a quotation about trench smells from an article by him in the *Observer* of 7 November 1958. The typical platoon was that of Alex Potter, whose detailed articles in the *Continental Daily Mail*, referred to in the text, he placed on loan – they were most useful. 'Tubby' Clayton's rat is mentioned in *Tales of Talbot House* (Toc H, 1919). For the training in France I used Blunden (quotation from p. 85), Sassoon's *Infantry Officer* (quotation from p. 15), 'Mark VII' (quoted) and *Death of a Hero*, Richard Aldington (Heinemann, 1929). Also Ian Hay's book for the useless raids. The anecdote about Wavell is from a biography by R. J. Collins (Hodder & Stoughton, 1947). The *Official History* (Vol.I.) and Cruttwell, for the administrative, air, mining, and supply preparations. *The Golden Virgin*, a documentary based on real experiences, gives some idea of other preparations and instructions. The pigeon story is from Lord Montgomery's *Memoirs* (Collins, 1958). The description of the giant mine crater at La Boisselle is from *An Onlooker in France* by Sir William Orpen (Williams & Norgate, 1924). Lloyd George's *War Memoirs* for Haig's selection of staff.

CHAPTER 8. Two books giving sensitive pictures of life in England in 1916, and well conveying the prevailing mood, are *Testament of Youth* (quotation from Part 2, Ch. 10) by Vera Brittain (Gollancz, 1933), and *Youth at the Gate* by Ursula Bloom (Hutchinson, 1959). I have consulted them both, and also newspapers, especially *The Times*. Asquith's reading matter is from *Memories and Reflections* (Vol. II).

CHAPTER 9. The *Official History* (Vol. I, notes to Chapters 3, 7, 8, 11, and 12); Cruttwell; *Encyclopaedia Americana; The Golden Virgin*. Falkenhayn gives an interesting account of the situation before the battle from the German point of view – his remark on reserves is quoted (p. 262). *Colossal Blunders of the War* (Allen & Unwin, 1930) by W. S. Woods was useful. The speeches of Henderson and Addison are from *The Times* of 2 June 1916. Masefield's *The Old Front Line* for the German positions, the strength of which is described and emphasized in many histories of the war, and in personal recollections. The *Official History* for the early attempts at camouflage.

CHAPTER 10. The *Official History* (Vol. I, Ch. 12), from which the reports of the four patrols; Masefields's *The Germans on the Somme* (quoted from p. 12) and *The Old Front Line*; Kabisch; Cruttwell; Lloyd George's *War Memoirs* (Ch. 19).

CHAPTER 11. The *Official History* (quotations from Vol. I, pp. 305, 314, 315); *The Golden Virgin;* Sassoon's *Infantry Officer* (quotations from pp. 68, 70, 72); Crozier (quotations from pp. 81, 82); Masefield's *The Somme* (quotations from pp. 8, 9, 11, 12, and 14); Haig's *Private Papers* (quotation from p. 151); Maurice; Charteris; Rawlinson's Operation Order from the *Official History* (Vol. I, p. 311); Gristwood.

CHAPTER 12. The *Official History* gives a detailed description of 1 July down to divisional level. *A Brass Hat in No Man's Land* (Cape, 1930) by F. P. Crozier (quotations from pp. 97 to 112). Sassoon's book again invaluable (quotations from pp. 75, 76, 77). Gristwood (quotation from p. 58). Masefield's *The Somme* (pp. 9, 10 quoted). Haig's *Private Papers* (pp. 153, 154, quoted). Also useful were Vera Brittain (*op. cit.*); Wavell's *Allenby: The Attack,* R. H. Tawney (Allen & Unwin, 1953); and Maurice (quoted). For the exploits of the Ulster Division, *The Irish on the Somme,* and Crozier's *The Men I Killed* (quotations from pp. 82 to 86). The losses of the 8th Division are from *The World Crisis* (p. 1077). M. St. H. Evans (quoted). *The Golden Virgin. The War Diaries of Albert I*, King of the Belgians, quoted here from p. 113 (Kimber, 1954), are full of wry comment on the progress of the war. There is a fine account of one sergeant's experiences on 1 July in *A Soldier's War* (privately, 1957), the diary of A. H. Cook, edited by Lt.-Gen. G. N. Molesworth.

CHAPTER 13. Girard; Pétain; Atteridge; Aston; *Encyclopaedia Americana*; Cruttwell; the *Official History* (Vol. II); Joffre.

CHAPTER 14. The *Official History* (Vol. I; the German official history quoted); Kabisch; *The Germans on the Somme*; *The World Crisis* (p. 1075 quoted); Falkenhayn (quoted); and Cruttwell.

CHAPTER 15. The *Official History* (Vol. II, p. 12 and *passim*). Haig's *Private Papers* (pp. 154, 156, 158, 160, 163 quoted). M. St. H. Evans (quoted at length); Sassoon's *Infantry Officer* (pp. 81, 83, 86, 88 quoted). Graves's *Goodbye to all That* (pp. 186, 187, 188, 189, 190, 192 quoted). Von Armin's report is from John Buchan's book. L. W. Griffith's *Up to Mametz* (quoted at length). The official report is from Haig's *Despatches*. Falkenhayn, and Maurice, again most helpful. J. A. Lawson's *Memories of Delville Wood* (quoted at length). *Anzac to Amiens*, especially the 3rd Battalion's plight (from p. 259). *Two Men I Knew* by C. E. W. Bean (Angus & Robertson, 1957), the official Australian historian, was useful for some of the Pozières material (quoted). Blunden; *A Subaltern on the Somme* (quoted); and Gristwood (p. 17 quoted). Masefield's *The Somme*. Hindenburg's remark I found in *Colossal Blunders of the War*. The regimental history of The King's Regiment (1954); 14 battalions of the regiment fought at the Somme.

CHAPTER 16. *The World Crisis* (pp. 510, 514 quoted); Lloyd George's *War Memoirs* (pp. 382, 383, 385 quoted); Haig's *Private Papers*; the *Official History* (especially the note to Ch. 9); Cruttwell; Liddell Hart's *The Tanks*, and *Reputations*. Two uncontroversial accounts of the beginnings of tanks are *Tank Warfare* by F. Mitchel (Nelson, 1933), and *Tanks in the Great War* by J. F. C. Fuller (John Murray, 1920).

CHAPTER 17. The *Official History* (Vol. II); Haig's *Private Papers* (pp. 166, 167 quoted); Lloyd George's *War Memoirs* (p. 323 quoted); *The World Crisis* (p. 525 quoted); Charteris (quoted); Liddell Hart's *The Tanks*; Vera Brittain; *The*

Times; Alex Potter's articles (quoted); *Soldiers and Statesmen* (p. 270 quoted); William George's book – a letter from his brother is quoted; M. St. H. Evans (quoted); *The Altar in the Loft* (Putnam, 1960; p. 132).

CHAPTER 18. Charteris; The *Official History* (Vol. II, quotations from pp. 469, 470); *A Subaltern on the Somme* (pp. 167-171); *A Subaltern's War* (description of the Butte quoted from p. 117); there is a quotation from A. A. Hanbury-Sparrow's *The Land-Locked Lake* (Barker, 1932; pp. 205, 210) – Hanbury-Sparrow was a Lt.-Col. in the 8th Division; *Undertones of War* by Blunden (state of dug-outs quoted from p. 139); Sir Arthur Sloggett's note is from *Northcliffe* (p. 512); the quotation from the General Staff's report is from *Soldiers and Statesmen*; the information about medals is from *A Subaltern on the Somme* (also quoted); Sassoon and Graves (quoted) were again most useful; the words at the chapter heading are from *The Times*, 10 November 1958.

CHAPTER 19. Haig's *Private Papers* (pp. 168, 172 quoted); the Northcliffe biography (his notes on Haig and the Somme are from p. 502); Charteris (his difficulties are from p. 162, the brandy story from p. 160); H. G. Wells (the quotation is from *The War and the Future*); the issue of the *Somme Times*, referred to was later collected into a volume, *The Wipers Times*, edited by Lt.-Col. F. J. Roberts; the description of Godbert's restaurant is quoted from *The Salient, the Somme and Arras*, by 'Bumble Bee' (1917; p. 59) – there is also a description of the place in Sassoon; Gristwood (quotation from p. 26); the comparatively comfortable life of an officer only just behind the line is also well illustrated in *War Letters of a Public-Schoolboy* by Paul Jones (Cassell, 1918).

CHAPTER 20. The *Official History*; F. M. Bridge's *History of the World War* (Deane, 1920); Haig's *Private Papers* (quotation from p. 175); Cruttwell; and Ludendorff (quoted).

CHAPTER 21. Girard; Joffre; Foch's biographers; Falkenhayn (p. 267 quoted); Ludendorff's *War Memoirs* (pp. 266, 278 quoted); Kabisch; *Guide to Military History of the World War* by T. G. Frothingham (Fisher Unwin, 1921).

CHAPTER 22. Haig's *Private Papers* (pp. 158 for Strachey, 168 for Gwynne, and 169 for Spender). The quotations from Dawson's book are selected from pp. 2 to 92. F. H. Keeling's letter is from his *Letters* (Allen & Unwin, 1918); Churchill's memo to F. E. Smith from *The World Crisis* (p. 184ff.).

CHAPTER 23. *The Man I Knew* (Haig's leave quoted). Haig's

Despatches (his views on machine-gunners quoted). Montgomery's *Memoirs* (his views on World War I Generals, p. 35). Lord Atlee's remark was made in a television interview on his 76th birthday. The official British and French casualty figures are from the British *Official History*. *Prelude to Victory* contains a long and fascinating description of the results of the German laying-waste policy in early 1917. Ludendorff (quoted). For the incredibly silly opposition of the cavalry to tanks *after* the war see *The Tanks*. There is a pen-portrait of the old battlefield in 1917, after the armies had moved on, in Christopher Hassall's *Edward Marsh* (Longmans, 1959). A description of the battlefield as it was between the wars is in Vera Brittain's *Testament of Friendship* (Macmillan, 1940). Strangely, however, the most moving and sensitive account of the old battlefield was written by an American, Scott Fitzgerald, in Book III of *Tender is the Night* (Penguin, 1955). But perhaps that is not so strange, after all ; for the Jazz Age itself was conceived at the graveyard of the age which preceded it.

Index

Addison, Dr, 63

Ainley, Henry, 61

Aitken, Sir William Maxwell (Lord Beaverbrook), 61, 160

Albert, 11, 32–3, 47, 49, 66, 74, 165

Albert, King of the Belgians, 96

Allenby, General Sir Edmund, 18, 27, 83; commands Third Army, 36, 37; and Haig, 37–8, 85

Amiens, 33, 149

Ancre Battle, 151–2

Ancre Heights, Battle of the, 139

Ancre Valley, 139

Arnim, General Sixt von, 115

Arras, 41, 42

Asquith, H. H., 15, 30–1, 37, 40, 61, 128, 132, 147–8, 159, 160

Asquith, Raymond, 134

Attlee, C. R. (Lord), 162

Auchonvilliers, 124

Australian Official History, quoted 119

Baden-Powell, Lady, 138

Bairnsfather, Bruce, 157

Baizieux, 149

Balfour, A. J., 27, 129, 145

Balfourier, General, 114

Bapaume, 11, 41, 165

Bazentin, 113

Bean, C. E. W., *Two Men I Knew*, quoted 121

Beaucourt, 152

Beaumont Hamel, 34, 66, 152

Beauquesne, 59, 77, 122

Beecham, Sir Thomas, 137

Below, General Fritz von, 62, 64, 102

Bernafay Wood, 66

Bernard, Colonel, 89–90

Bing Boys, 138

Birdwood, Lord, 121

Blunden, Edmund, 52, 108, 124; quoted 142–3

Boraston, J. H., 163

Briand, A., 25, 27, 35, 40

Bridges, General, 124

British Army

THIRD ARMY, 36, 37, 65

FOURTH ARMY

Corps: III, 91; VII, 83, 85, 94, 96; VIII, 86–8, 95–6; X, 88, 91, 95; XIII, 92–3, 100, 102;

British Army – *contd.*
    XV, 91, 92; Anzac, 119
    Divisions: 4th, 69; 8th, 91; 19th, 124; 29th, 70; 30th, 93; 36th (Ulster), 75, 88–90; 42nd, 64; 46th, 86; 56th (London), 85; South African, 115
    Regiments and Battalions: Bedfordshires, 135; Deccan Horse, 115; Dragoon Guards, 115; East Lancashires, 87; East Yorkshires, 92; Green Howards, 92; Middlesex, 91; Royal Irish Rifles, 94; Royal Ulster Rifles, 127; Royal Welch Fusiliers, 108, 109, 116; South African Brigade, 20th, 116; South Staffordshires, 92; Suffolks, 116; West Yorkshires, 92; York and Lancasters, 87, 91
    FIFTH ARMY, 95, 119, 122, 139, 151–2
British Expeditionary Force, 13
Brittain, Vera, 60
Brusilov, General, 22
Buchan, John, 157
Buckingham Bullet, 53
'Bumble Bee', *The Salient, the Somme and Arras*, quoted 149–50
Butte de Warlencourt, 140–1
Bystander, 43

Cambridge, Duke of, 20
Carrington, C. E. ('Charles Edmonds') quoted 140–1
Carson, Lord, 29
Casement, Sir Roger, 61
Castelnau, General de, 25
Chantilly, 16, 160
Charteris, Brigadier-General, 16, 17, 41, 59, 77, 139, 146, 147; quoted, 135, 144, 147
Churchill, Winston, 14, 18, 27–8, 38, 44, 122; quoted 102–3; and tanks, 128–30, 131–2, 136; memorandum to F. E. Smith, 159
Clayton, 'Tubby', 51
Contalmaison, 38
Courcelette, 136
Crozier, Colonel F. P., 75; quoted 79–80, 89–90, 94
Crucifix Valley, 66
Curragh mutiny, 13, 39

Daily Mail, 61
Dare, Phyllis, 14
Dawson, Captain A. J., *Somme Battle Stories*, quoted 157–8
Delville Wood, 11, 66, 115–18, 122
Derby, Lord, 29, 160
des Vallières, General, 23
Dowding, Lord, 56
du Maurier, Gerald, 137
Duval, Colonel, 99

Edmonds, J. E., 162
Eisenhower, Dwight D., 162
Étaples, 47
Evans, Lieut. M. St. Helier,
    quoted 96, 107–8, 123–4,
    138

Falkenhayn, General, 21, 22,
    26, 63, 64, 104, 112, 154,
    155
Fayolle, General, 99, 153
Flers, 135, 136
Flixécourt, 52
Foch, General, 18, 25, 27,
    106, 134; his objections
    to Somme attack, 35–6,
    41; and the battle, 99,
    101, 106–7; relieved of
    command, 153
Frankau, Gilbert, 148
French, Sir John, 13, 15, 20,
    36, 44
French Army
    SIXTH
    XX Corps ('Iron Corps')
    99, 100, 114; XXXV
    Corps, 99; I Colonial
    Corps, 99, 100
    TENTH, 153
Freyberg, Lieut.-Colonel B.
    C. (later Lord), 152
Fricourt, 34, 62, 66, 80, 91,
    92, 105

Gallipoli, 14, 28
George V, King, 20, 29–30,
    37, 40, 122
German Sixth Army, 62–3
Gibbs, Philip, 156, 157

Girard, G., 163
Godbert's   restaurant,
    Amiens, 149–50
Gommecourt, 34, 36, 62,
    64, 70, 94
Gommecourt Salient, 85, 86
Gough, Lieut.-General Sir
    Hubert, 13, 39, 58, 95,
    105, 115, 118–21, 139,
    149, 151
Graves, Robert, 55, 108, 142;
    quoted 50, 51, 117–18,
    143–4
Griffith, L. W., Up to Mametz,
    quoted 111, 124–5
Gristwood, A. D., quoted
    82, 125–6, 150
Grock, 137
Guillemont, 122
Guinchy, 136
Gwynne, Stephen, 156

Haig, General Sir Douglas,
    15, 16, 44, 54, 63, 71,
    115, 149; and the plan of
    offensive, 16–18; charac-
    ter, and earlier career,
    19–20; and Verdun, 24;
    and Joffre, 24–5; and
    Lloyd George, 28–9; and
    Robertson, 30; his plan,
    35, 36, 41–2; and
    Allenby, 37–8, 85; and
    Kitchener's death, 39–
    40; and preparations for
    the battle, 58–9; his
    'yes-men', 59; his con-
    fidence, 77; sees Raw-
    linson, 83; instructs

Haig, General Sir Douglas
– contd.
Rawlinson to continue attack, 95; on the failure of VIII Corps, 96; plans to continue attack, 105; persuades Joffre to accept his views, 106; and Mametz Wood, 108; agrees to night attack, 113; orders capture of Pozières, 119, 120, 122; and a war of attrition, 121, 122, 127; and the King's visit, 122; and use of tanks, 130–2; and Lloyd George's visits, 133–4, 145; his other visitors, 145–7; on leaves, 160; confers with Joffre, 160; supporters and detractors of, 161–2; on the Somme casualties, 163; honours, and final years, 167

Haig, Lady, 40, 41, 160
Haldane, R. B. (Lord), 13, 14, 20
Hampshire, H.M.S., 29, 40
Hanbury-Sparrow, A. A., *The Land-Locked Lake*, quoted 142
Hawthorn Redoubt, 86
Henderson, Arthur, 63
High Wood, 66, 114, 115, 118, 122, 136
Hindenburg, 113, 154
Hindenburg Line, 163

Howell-Price, Lieut.-Colonel O., 120
Hunter-Weston, General, 87, 96

Joffre, General, 14, 15, 35, 36, 40, 41, 54, 101, 121, 130, 139; plan of offensive, 16–18; characteristics, 18–19; and Verdun, 21, 24; and Haig, 24–5; presses for Somme attack, 25–6; accepts Haig's views, 106; and cavalry, 134; replaced by Nivelle, 153; confers with Haig, 160–1
Jones, David, 108, 144
Jutland, Battle of, 60

Kaiser, the, 21, 22, 62
Keane, Doris, 61
Keeling, F. H., quoted 158
Kiggell, Lieut.-General L. E., 59, 113
Kitchener, Lord, 14, 15, 18–20, 27–9, 40, 43, 44, 69

La Boisselle, 66, 91, 107
Law, A. Bonar, 40, 61, 160
Lawson, J. A., *Memories of Delville Wood*, 116–17
Leipzig Salient, 66, 88
Le Sars, 139
Lewis Gun, 53
Little Tich, 137
Lloyd George, D., 15, 19,

27, 28, 63, 69, 112, 122, 138, 159, 161, 163; and Haig, 28–9; Secretary for War, 30; and tanks, 129, 130, 132, 135; visits to the Front, 133–4, 145–6; Prime Minister, 160

Longueval, 105, 113, 122

Loos, 15, 135

Ludendorff, General Erich, 152, 154–5, 163, 165

Mametz Wood, 11, 34, 66, 91, 92, 108–12

Marne, 19

Martinpuich, 136

Masefield, John, 70, 75–6, 82, 108, 157

Matthews, A. E., 137

Meaulte, 150

Messines, Battle of, 69

Michel, General, 13

Micheler, General, 153

Millar, Gertie, 61

Monchy-Breton, 51

Mons, 14

Montagu, Edwin, 132, 148

Montague, C. E., 107

Montauban, 34, 97

Montenegro, King of, 147

Montgomery, Lord, 53, 162; quoted 57–8

Montreuil, 59

Morning Post, 156

Mouquet Farm, 122, 136

Mutiny in French Army, 22

Nancy, 99

Nares, Owen, 61

Neuve Chapelle, 15, 36

Nivelle, General, 153

Northcliffe, Lord, 29–30, 143; quoted 146–7

Northcote, Hon. Mrs. G., 61

Noyon Salient, 32, 35

Official German History of the War, 162

Official History (British), quoted 71, 72, 74–5, 87, 95, 105–7, 124, 141–2

Oman, Sir Charles, 162

Orpen, Sir William, 56

Ovillers, 66, 91, 107

Passchendaele, 141, 161

Peronne, 32

Pétain, General, 22, 25

Pinney, Major-General R. J., 142

Plowman, Mark, 108; quoted 52, 125–7, 140, 144

Plumer, General, 27

Poincaré, President, 25, 35, 117

Potter, Alex, *Memories of a Kitchener's Man*, quoted 45, 51

Pozières, 34, 38, 106, 119–20, 122, 147

Querrieux, 59, 83

Rawlinson, General Sir Henry, 18, 27, 46, 59, 68, 83; leads main attack

Rawlinson, General Sir Henry
– contd.
36, 37; career and
character, 38; his ob-
jections to Haig's plan,
38–9; his *Tactical Notes*,
55; last message to
troops, 67, 77; and the
first day of battle, 95;
and Mametz Wood, 108;
launches night attack,
113, 114
Robertson, Sir William, 29,
30, 131, 137
Robey, George, 61
Robinson, H. P., 156, 157
Royal Flying Corps, 55–6;
bombing rôle, 68
Royal Naval Division, 152
Rupprecht of Bavaria, Crown
Prince, 62–4, 151, 154

St. Pierre Divion, 88
St. Quentin, 165
Sassoon, Sir Philip, 146
Sassoon, Siegfried, 52;
quoted 71–4, 80–1, 95,
108, 109
Schwaben Redoubt, 88, 94,
136, 142
Serre, 34, 86, 87, 95, 96, 152
Sherriff, R. C., 148
Sitwell, Osbert, 122
Sloggett, Sir Arthur, 143
Smith, F. E. (Lord Birkenhead), 27, 159
Somervell, D. C., 18
Somme, Battle of the: the
French press for attack,
24–6; the Old Front
Line, 32–4; Haig's plan,
35, 39; Foch's objec-
tions, 35–6; the British
generals, 36–8; Rawlin-
son's objections, 38–9;
preparations for the
battle, 43–59; German
expectations, 62–4; Ger-
man positions, 64–7;
artillery bombardment,
68–70; discharge of gas,
68–9; patrols and raid-
ing parties, 71–2; the
Operation Order, 72–3;
getting on parade, 73–8;
the first day, 79–98; the
French sector, 99–101;
the infantry assault, 102–
4; the attack continued,
105–8; Mametz Wood,
108–12; night attack,
113–14; Delville Wood
and High Wood, 115–
18; attack on Pozières,
119–22; the battle of
attrition, 122–7; misuse
of tanks, 133–8; Trans-
loy Ridges and Ancre
Heights, 139–44; scenes
behind the lines, 145–
50; the Ancre Battle,
151–2; the rôle of the
French, 153; effect on
the Germans, 154–5;
the argument over the
battle, 161–2; casualties,
162–3; the German re-
treat, 163, 165

Somme Times, 148–9

Spectator, 156

Spender, J. A., 157

Steed, Wickham, 146

Strachey, J. St. Loe, 156

Swinton, E. D., 128, 129, 131

Tate, Harry, 61

Thiepval, 11, 34, 70, 88, 106, 127, 143; Thiepval Salient, 119, 122

Times, The, 61, 156

Transloy Ridges, Battle of the, 139

Trenchard, Major-General H. M., 56

Trones Wood, 66, 113

Vanbrugh, Irene, 61

Verdun, 21–6, 35, 63, 99, 101, 106, 130, 137, 153, 154

Wavell, Lord, 53, 64, 162

Wells, H. G., 128, 148

Westminster Gazette, 157

Williamson, Henry, quoted 48

Wilson, Woodrow, 161

Wood, Sir Henry, 137

Ypres, 15, 27

James Clavell
TAI-PAN

Now only 10/6
705 Pages

In this turbulent, panoramic novel of the
founding of Hong Kong, James Clavell, author of
KING RAT, narrates the saga of how one
man, with majestic vision, ruthless will and
ingenious grasp of command, guides the development
of a colony destined to influence the course
of history. It is a masterful re-creation
of a momentous epoch in the history
of the British Empire.

SPHERE BOOKS INCLUDE:
(arranged by subject)

BIOGRAPHY & AUTOBIOGRAPHY

A SILVER-PLATED SPOON	Duke of Bedford	5/-
MARLBOROUGH – VOLUME 1	Winston S. Churchill	12/6
MARLBOROUGH – VOLUME 2	Winston S. Churchill	12/6
MARLBOROUGH – VOLUME 3	Winston S. Churchill	12/6
MARLBOROUGH – VOLUME 4	Winston S. Churchill	12/6
MARLBOROUGH – VOL. 1/2/3/4	Winston S. Churchill	
in presentation case		50/-
I'LL COME BACK IN THE SPRINGTIME	Maurice N. Hennessy	5/-

DOMESTIC SCIENCE

GREAT DISHES OF THE WORLD	Robert Carrier	10/6

GENERAL FICTION

THE CONSCIENCE OF LOVE	Marcel Ayme	4/-
SPELLA HO	H. E. Bates	5/-
FLIGHT OF FATE	Vicki Baum	4/-
THE WEEPING WOOD	Vicki Baum	7/6
THE HOUSE IN PARIS	Elizabeth Bowen	4/-
ATLAN	Jane Gaskell	5/-
THE CITY	Jane Gaskell	5/-
THE SERPENT	Jane Gaskell	5/-
THE BLAZE OF NOON	Rayner Heppenstall	4/-
ALL THE CONSPIRATORS	Christopher Isherwood	3/6
RETREAT TO INNOCENCE	Doris Lessing	5/-
TROUBLE IN BURMA	Van Wyck Mason	3/6
CONFESSIONS OF A MASK	Yukio Mishima	4/-
APPOINTMENT WITH VENUS	Jerrard Tickell	3/6
THE DEATH SHIP	B. Traven	6/-
A STANDARD OF BEHAVIOUR	William Trevor	3/6

HISTORY

A SHORT HISTORY OF THE RUSSIAN REVOLUTION	Joel Carmichael	5/-

MYSTERY & THRILLER

THE MAN WHO CHOSE DEATH	Eric Allen	4/-
DEVIL BY THE SEA	Nina Bawden	4/-
THE SOLITARY CHILD	Nina Bawden	4/-
DOUBLE FOR THE TOFF	John Creasey	3/6
HERE COMES THE TOFF	John Creasey	3/6
THE TOFF PROCEEDS	John Creasey	3/6
THE TOFF TO MARKET	John Creasey	3/6
CABLE CAR	June Drummond	3/6
CALL AFTER MIDNIGHT	M. G. Eberhart	3/6
RUN SCARED	M. G. Eberhart	3/6
THE DISAPPEARING BRIDEGROOM	Margaret Erskine	3/6
THE WHISPERING HOUSE	Margaret Erskine	3/6
THE CASE OF THE LUCKY LEGS	Erle Stanley Gardner	2/6

THE CASE OF THE SULKY GIRL	Erle Stanley Gardner	2/6
THE CASE OF THE VELVET CLAWS	Erle Stanley Gardner	2/6
CLUE OF THE FORGOTTEN MURDER	Erle Stanley Gardner	2/6
THE D.A. CALLS A TURN	Erle Stanley Gardner	2/6
THE D.A. COOKS A GOOSE	Erle Stanley Gardner	2/6
THE D.A. GOES TO TRIAL	Erle Stanley Gardner	2/6
THE HOURS AFTER MIDNIGHT	Joseph Hayes	3/6

POLITICAL SCIENCE & ECONOMICS

THE BITTER HERITAGE	Arthur Schlesinger	5/–

REFERENCE & GUIDE

PEARS MEDICAL ENCYCLOPAEDIA	J. A. C. Brown	7/6

ROMANCE

THE MAN BEHIND THE MASK	Patricia Robins	3/6

SCIENCE FICTION

FAR BOUNDARIES	August Derleth	3/6
THE ODIOUS ONES	Jerry Sohl	3/6
THE TIME DISSOLVER	Jerry Sohl	4/–

SELF HELP

YOGA OVER FORTY	Michael Volin & Nancy Phelan	5/–

SOCIAL SCIENCE

THE SECOND OSWALD	R. H. Popkin	4/6

TRAVEL & ADVENTURE

ULYSSES FOUND	Ernle Bradford	4/6
THE SLAVES OF TIMBUKTU	Robin Maugham	5/–

WAR BOOKS

THE FACE OF WAR	Martha Gellhorn	5/–
THE WAR GAME (Illus.)	Peter Watkins	5/–

WESTERNS

DESERT HERITAGE	Zane Grey	3/6
LIGHT OF THE WESTERN STARS	Zane Grey	3/6
PRAIRIE GOLD	Zane Grey	3/6
THE RAINBOW TRAIL	Zane Grey	3/6
RIDERS OF VENGEANCE	Zane Grey	3/6
THIEVES' CANYON	Zane Grey	3/6
WILD FIRE	Zane Grey	3/6

J.A.C. Brown
Pears Medical Encyclopaedia

7/6

555 Pages

This newly revised edition of a famous household
reference work is as interesting as a novel
and as informative as its sister volume,
PEARS CYCLOPAEDIA. It covers the wide range of
Medical Matters, relates modern medicine to its
social background and talks sheer good
sense on many controversial and taboo topics.

The new edition includes many entries dealing
with contemporary problems. The Pill is here,
so is E.C.T., "Fringe Medicine", the population
explosion, lung cancer, tranquilisers and drug
addiction. But perhaps its most valuable
quality is its commonsense approach to everyday
anxieties about health.